HMS *Belfast* during a British fleet visit to the IJ in Amsterdam, 1962. (Public domain)

CONTENTS

Cover image: HMS *Belfast* during the Korean War, c. 1950–51. (Author's collection)

Library of Congress Cataloging-in-Publication Data is available.
ISBN: 978-1-68247-982-7 (print)
ISBN: 978-1-68247-998-8 (eBook)

HMS *Belfast* clears the slipway on 17 March 1938. As was typical of warship construction of this period, she lacks armament and most of the superstructure, which would be installed during the fitting-out phase prior to commissioning. (Public domain)

INTRODUCTION

HMS *Belfast* was the last of the "full-size" British "Treaty" cruisers; all others constructed after her were built in compliance with the limitations imposed by the Second London Naval Treaty or derivations therefrom. While numerous "improved *Belfast*" and other large cruiser designs would be drawn up, none were ever laid down, let alone completed.

Her career started just before World War II, and initially it seemed that it would be a relatively short one. Heavily damaged by a magnetic mine, she was given a reprieve only because of her brand-new status. But from there she went on to take part in numerous critical battles and campaigns: chasing down German battleships, supporting the largest amphibious landings the world has ever seen, holding the line in the crucial weeks when Korea's future hung in the balance, and then surviving long enough to become the largest museum ship in the United Kingdom.

Her survival was in large part thanks to her unique capabilities, themselves largely granted by the extensive repair work done in the drydocks where she was restored after the fateful encounter with the mine. Without that mine impact and subsequent reconstruction, she likely would have been disposed of much sooner or else been in too poor a state to preserve come the 1970s. Fate often turns on such strange incidents.

This work is based on a large range of documents, including a number of preexisting books covering either the ship, her class, or British cruisers generally in World War II and thereafter. Additionally, the National Archives at Kew, England, and the Royal Navy Archives at Portsmouth were invaluable in resolving questions raised in conflicting accounts pertaining to *Belfast*'s operational records. Also invaluable have been the hundreds of hours of oral history recorded over the years and maintained by the Imperial War Museum. The voices of some of those who served on board her are preserved there, and a select number of accounts have been partially transcribed to give an idea of what it was like to serve on board *Belfast*.

Of course, the ship herself was an invaluable aid in developing this book. She sits on the River Thames in London, just upriver from Tower Bridge, and was a frequent destination during the writing process because some details must be seen before they can be described in text. As this is a popular work and in line with the other books in this series, specific sourcing is not present in this volume. Readers who would like to know where a particular item of information came from are welcome to get in touch with the author.

At the time of writing HMS *Belfast* is due to see a namesake successor in the form of a modern Type 26 frigate enter service before the end of the decade. As you are about to discover, the new ship and her crew have big shoes to fill.

A TREATY CRUISER IN A POST-TREATY WORLD

HMS *Belfast* was the last of the Town-class cruisers commissioned. She was laid down shortly before her sister HMS *Edinburgh*, but the latter was commissioned almost a full month before her. Although *Belfast* officially entered service weeks before the outbreak of World War II, her origins lay half a decade in the past, when a system of naval treaties had governed the design of warships. Those days were a far cry from the environment the new ship found herself thrust into; indeed, throughout her life *Belfast* would find herself facing almost every situation imaginable for a light cruiser except the one for which she was actually designed.

DEVELOPMENT

The Town-class ships had their origins in the development of the newly minted "light cruiser" category, a warship designation that did not exist until the 1930 London Naval Treaty (although the term "light armoured cruiser," sometimes shortened to "light cruiser," was in use during World War I) split the "cruiser" category defined in the Washington Naval Treaty into a limited number of ships armed with 8-inch/203-mm guns and a larger number that would be permitted guns no larger than 6.1-inch/155-mm. While ships with this lower calibre of gun had existed in the past, they had mainly been conceived as facing off against others of their kind when serving as fleet scouts or lesser vessels such as destroyers or armed merchant ships in commerce raiding or protection roles. Larger armoured cruisers with bigger guns were considered significantly superior, as their guns' destructive power far exceeded that of a 6-inch shell, and the rates of fire between the different-sized weapons were not different enough to give the smaller ship any real advantage, quite apart from the fact the larger ships usually carried an extensive secondary battery that typically matched the smaller ships' main battery on its own.

However, with advances in gun technology during the 1920s and early 1930s, the rate of fire and overall lethality of the 6-inch gun had increased dramatically. Combined with a 10,000-ton maximum standard displacement limit that was already forcing difficult compromises to be made in the balance of speed, protection, and firepower—not to mention endurance and a number of other factors—it seemed that the 6-inch light cruiser might stand a chance against a similarly sized heavy cruiser if she could bring enough shells to bear quickly enough to overwhelm her opponent before the latter's larger shells could deal fatal damage. Somewhat ironically, a "hail of fire" from 6-inch weapons had been posited as a battle-winning formula back in the 1890s when the first quick-firing (QF) guns had been installed on warships. Nonetheless, the Royal Navy still viewed the 6-inch-armed light cruiser as primarily a weapon of commerce warfare, to be used either to protect British and Allied ships against

HMS *Belfast* approaching completion in early 1939. The 4-inch AA guns are yet to be installed, but the superstructure is largely complete. (Author's collection)

TABLE 2.1. COMPARISON OF 1930s CRUISERS OF THE IMPERIAL JAPANESE, UNITED STATES, AND ROYAL NAVIES

	Mogami	***Brooklyn***	**Town-class**	***Belfast*** **(as built)**
Displacement (standard)	c. 11,000 tons	c. 9,750 tons	c. 8,950–9,400 tons	c. 10,900 tons
Main battery	15 x 6.1-inch/155-mm (5 x triple turrets)	15 x 6-inch/152-mm (5 x triple turrets)	12 x 6-inch/152-mm (4 x triple turrets)	12 x 6-inch/152-mm (4 x triple turrets)
Secondary/heavy AA battery	8 x 5-inch/127-mm (4 x twin mounts)	8 x 5-inch/127-mm (8 x single mounts)	8 x 4-inch/102-mm (4 x twin mounts)	12 x 4-inch/102-mm (6 x twin mounts)
Light/medium AA battery	4 x 40-mm (4 x single mounts)	8 x 0.50-caliber machine guns (8 x single mounts)	8 x 40-mm (2 x quad mounts) 8 x 0.50-caliber machine guns (2 x quad mounts)	8 x 40-mm (2 x quad mounts) 8 x 0.50-caliber machine guns (2 x quad mounts)
Torpedoes	12 x 24-inch/610-mm (4 x triple tube launchers)	none	6 x 21-inch/533-mm (2 x triple tube launchers)	6 x 21-inch/533-mm (2 x triple tube launchers)
Top speed	37 knots	32.5 knots	c. 32 knots	32 knots
Armour: belt	5.5-inch/140-mm (magazines) 3.9-inch/100-mm (elsewhere)	2-inch/51-mm (magazines) 5-inch/127-mm (elsewhere)	4.5-inch/114-mm	4.5-inch/114-mm
Armour: deck	1.4-inch/35-mm	2-inch/51-mm	1.5-inch/38-mm	3-inch/76-mm
Armour: turrets	1-inch/25-mm	6.5-inch/165-mm (face)	1-inch/25-mm or 4-inch/102-mm (depending on sub-class)	4-inch/102-mm

enemy raiders or to conduct raiding of their own when the opportunity arose.

Ostensibly following the terms of the London Treaty, Japan developed the *Mogami* class, which was armed with no fewer than five triple 6-inch turrets for a total of 15 barrels. The United States constructed the *Brooklyn* class, similarly armed in terms of the main battery but without torpedo launchers. In the United Kingdom the result was the Town class in its initial *Southampton* variant. The latter was armed with 12 guns in 4 triple turrets, 3 guns fewer than the *Mogami* and *Brooklyn* classes, but like the Japanese vessel carried torpedoes. The main reason that neither the American nor the British ships could match the *Mogami*'s on-paper capabilities was simple: both nations were building to the treaty's limits, but the Japanese were not, and so could accommodate a wider range of weapons on their ships. Somewhat ironically, as it turned out, the Japanese had no intention of keeping the *Mogamis* as light (or Type B) cruisers, having designed them for conversion to heavy (Type A) cruisers by swapping out the triple 6-inch turrets for twin 8-inch versions. The reason Japan built the ships with 155-mm guns was simply to give the appearance of following the treaty restrictions until it would be too late for other navies to match their suddenly enlarged fleet of more heavily gunned warships, at least in theory.

But all of that was in the future in the mid-1930s. For the present the Royal Navy wanted a ship capable of going toe-to-toe with the newest light cruisers and many of the 8-inch-armed heavy cruisers as well and believed the Town class was the solution—at least at first.

There had been a little bit of "spare" tonnage in the Town-class design as built, compared with the 10,000-ton upper limit the Royal Navy was still following. But as more and more of the 15-gun ships

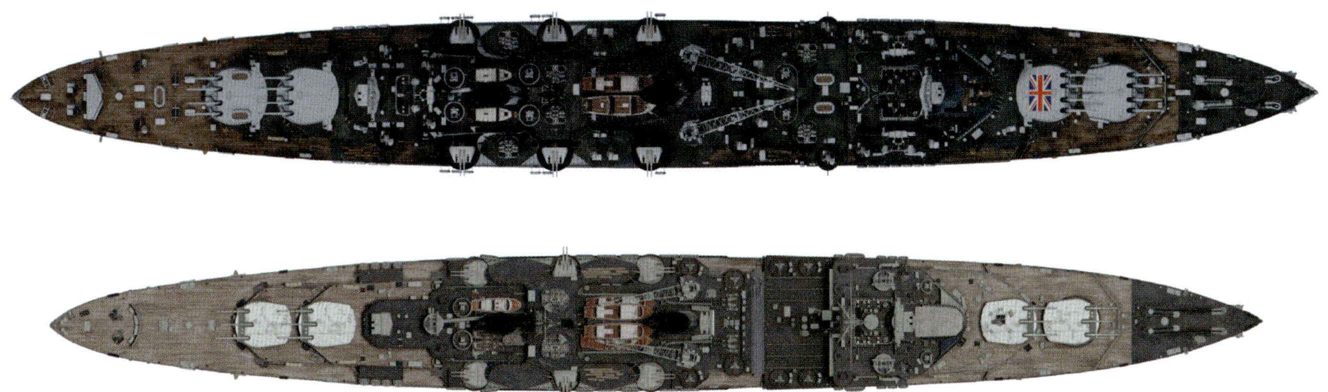

The 4-gun and final 3-gun layouts; the general layout remained largely the same between the two. (Ship models from World of Warships, arranged by Ryan P)

began to enter service on both sides of the Pacific, the Royal Navy was determined to match that number. A revised Town-class design was prepared, but designers realized quickly that adding a fifth triple turret was unworkable if the other features of the ship and proposed improvements were to be retained. Instead work went into developing a quadruple 6-inch turret. Four of these would give the revised ship a 16-gun salvo—one more than her contemporaries had—while also retaining torpedo-launching facilities, armour protection, and a 32-knot speed at just about 10,000 tons. This would represent a better-engineered vessel than the Japanese ship, which British designers already suspected was either significantly overweight or else dangerously lightly built (it was both), and would point the way to potential future light cruiser designs.

As it turned out, fitting four guns into a marginally larger turret produced unacceptable interference between the various shells' flight paths, and this, along with other issues surrounding the rate of fire, led to the abandonment of the idea after several gun layouts were tried with little success. The new ship design reverted to four triple turrets, but with various minor improvements compared with the "stock" Town class. By the second half of the 1930s it was also evident that the naval treaty system was collapsing, and designers were given a slightly freer hand regarding the ships' final displacement. Larger displacements led to a number of other design changes before the ships took their final form.

HMS *Belfast* fitting out in 1938. The offset of the funnels compared with those of older Town-class cruisers is quite apparent. (Author's collection)

THE MAKING OF A MODERN LIGHT CRUISER

Starting out in the interwar period as an idea for a "death ray," radar rapidly developed into a somewhat more feasible detection, as opposed to destruction, system—one whose deployment and capability tracked closely with *Belfast*'s own operational history. The British "Type" designation of this period reflects both wartime security measures and the many types of radar available, so the number sequence of the radars does not always represent technological advancement. The appearance of Type 262 radar considerably later than Type 271, for example, does not represent a backward step in ships' equipment. Certain kinds of radar such as air search were much easier to develop than accurate gunnery control units because of the different requirements of each. As time went on and more and more radar units came into use, they competed for space on board navy ships. *Belfast* at various points carried more than half the main naval radars produced. A quick summary of the main roles of radar is useful.

AIR SEARCH

The first radar fitted to naval vessels (specifically a Type 79 set fitted to *Belfast*'s half-sister, HMS *Sheffield*), air search (or "air warning") radar scanned the skies for returns that indicated the presence of aircraft. Able to see far beyond the visual range of human eyes, air search radar gave advanced warning of an incoming attack and allowed the ship to make ready, take evasive action, request support, or direct other friendly units to intercept. As time went on, air search radar, was refined and could scan farther distances with greater clarity, improving the quality of the information received. At shorter distances it was discovered that it could also

Type 974 surface search radar is still on board the ship. (Imperial War Museum)

Type 281 air search radar was installed in 1942 and not removed until 1959. (Imperial War Museum)

pick up large objects emerging out of the sea, which in turn led to the development of surface search radar.

SURFACE SEARCH

While it had considerably shorter spotting range than air search and was limited by the physical horizon (the wavelengths it employed were incapable of following the curve of the earth, and water is effectively opaque to radar in general), surface search radar was highly useful for several reasons. Although a pair of good eyes and top-of-the-range lenses might allow a spotter to see the same thing on a good day, radar didn't get tired, and it could see through fog, sea spray, snow, rain, and darkness (in naval terms night is a kind of weather) that humans struggled to deal with. A ship equipped with surface search radar could detect, monitor, and then either evade, track, or engage another vessel undetected unless that vessel had equally capable radar of her own or a radar warning receiver. Although it could be confused by a mass of returns if pointed at a coastline, in the open seas surface search radar was a game-changar. *Belfast* used it to good effect at the Battle of the North Cape, tracking and following the battleship *Scharnhorst* in weather that otherwise would likely have allowed the German ship to escape.

GUNNERY CONTROL

While data from air search and surface search radars could give an idea of range and bearing for use in gunnery fire control, the accuracy of the data and rapidity of its transmission were not generally good enough for anything more than approximate values. Refined versions of these longer-range radars were supplemented, and in many cases later replaced, by specialized units that could provide continuous high-fidelity information to a ship's main fire control director for the main battery, or to local fire control units for the antiaircraft battery. Toward the end of World War II these radar units became small enough to be installed on individual weapon mounts, giving each emplacement its own electronic fire control capability. In order to accomplish this gunnery control, units usually sacrificed range and were focused on a single bearing—straight at the target—which meant that ships had to be equipped with surface- and air-focused gunnery control units in addition to, rather than instead of, the wider-ranging search/warning sets.

Type 285 gunnery radar was only replaced in the ship's last refit. (Public Domain)

It should also be noted that for a considerable portion of World War II, radar screens did not look anything like the modern circular screen with distinct dots of light popping up on it. Rather the screen looked more like an oscilloscope with various peaks along a line. The radar plan position indicator was introduced mid-war and more closely resembled the radar screen of today, its more distinct data being a significant improvement.

The advent of aircraft in military roles during World War I had not been unappreciated by navies, but aircraft carriers were generally large, rare, and expensive, thus unlikely to be on call in every possible place and time a cruiser or other ship might find herself. In early experiments on battleships, a wheeled aircraft was installed on a small take-off ramp fitted to a turret, and while these provided limited scouting and defence capabilities, they also were one-use machines because there was no way to recover them. Ditching nearby was perilous for the pilot if the weather was bad or a destroyer wasn't on hand to pluck him from the water.

The ship's Walrus aircraft approaching, 1939. The type was commonly used in the Royal Navy but had a relatively brief active career on *Belfast*. (Imperial War Museum)

One potential solution was the seaplane, an aircraft that could land on water and then be craned back aboard, at least in moderate seas, to be used again. Unfortunately, the floats hindered the aircraft's performance, and the brief era of the surface warship with its own air defence capability (even if somewhat limited) rapidly came to an end. The aircraft available for use by noncarrier warships were thus largely restricted to air search and gunnery spotting roles, although they were still incredibly useful because they extended the ship's "eyes" well over the horizon, potentially for hundreds of miles, and afforded more rapid correction of gunnery. Spotters also allowed ships to fire over low-lying obstacles such as land outcrops and through smokescreens or fog—as long as the enemy's antiaircraft fire or their own seaplanes didn't interfere too much!

As time went on, some such aircraft, whether by design or field modification, were also able to take on a light strike role with small bombs and such defensive armament as they possessed, usually hunting submarines or poorly defended land targets of opportunity. The balance of roles and the capacity of the ship reflected greatly in the aircraft assigned to different vessels, not just between navies but even within navies. Smaller British cruisers carried the Fairey Seafox; larger ships, including *Belfast*, were able to operate larger aircraft such as a floatplane version of the Fairey Swordfish or—for *Belfast* specifically—the Supermarine Walrus, a pusher-engined biplane flying boat with a waterproof hull. These aircraft, fitted with wheels in case they had to land ashore or on a carrier, had no pretensions to aerial combat but were very useful for their endurance in the aerial spotting role and their ability to go after the occasional U-boat caught on the surface. *Belfast* was able to carry two aircraft but operated them only during the brief period between her commission and being mined, and then after reentering service to mid-1943.

Aircraft and their associated equipment, supplies, and storage took up a lot of space and weight on a ship, especially a cruiser such as *Belfast*. While this was tolerated as long as the planes were useful, by the middle of World War II radar had taken over most of the roles that the Walrus had previously fulfilled, and in June 1943 the aircraft on board were sent to other duties. A few ships retained at least one aircraft. Radar was capable of many things, but air-sea rescue was not one of them; as carrier operations became more and more frequent, many a pilot forced to ditch was grateful to see a friendly Walrus wandering up to him. The aircraft's excellent low-speed handling and its backup landing gear also meant these rescued men could be delivered back to their carrier because a Walrus could land on a carrier's flight deck without the need for arrestor gear or other such devices, then head back on patrol or to its home ship.

Equipped with four boilers driving four turbine units (themselves split into High Power and Lower Power sets) and with a rated power output of 80,000 shaft horsepower (shp) (reduced from an initially proposed 82,500 shp on efficiency grounds), *Belfast* was designed to be capable of 32 knots, although more typically she cruised at lower speeds and had a longer range than the older Town class because she carried several hundred tons more oil fuel. She proved to be slightly faster than expected, reaching almost 33 knots on one of her trial runs.

Their machinery layout made *Belfast* and *Edinburgh* easy to distinguish from their predecessors. The boiler and engine rooms were moved considerably aft to shorten the propeller shafts, the designers believing that a longer propeller shaft was more likely to be bent out of shape if the ship were struck by magnetic-influence torpedoes or a B bomb. This meant the funnels were positioned farther back as well to avoid unneeded additional trunking under the decks. Thus, the aft funnel was just forward of the aft superstructure while the fore funnel sat neatly amidships behind the aircraft launching facilities. This structural change would prove fortunate. It almost certainly made the difference between survival and loss for *Belfast* early in her career.

THE B BOMB

The more intense effect of underwater explosions on ships compared with internal or above-water detonations was already well known by the time *Belfast* was being designed. Quite apart from the obvious fact that it is easier to sink a ship by letting water in the bottom than by letting air in the top, the incompressible (for most purposes) nature of water tends to confine and direct explosions adjacent to or near a ship in a way that ensures greater destructive effects than the exact same explosion would have if it took place in open air.

Because of this and the limited payload of many strike aircraft tasked with antishipping missions in the 1930s, the British developed the 250-pound Buoyancy Bomb, or B Bomb, which was designed to be dropped not *on* ships but *in front* of them. The B Bomb outwardly resembled a relatively conventional bomb except with a blunt nose (this gave the weapon better underwater ballistics than a pointed end). When the bomb hit the water, the blunt nose dished in and the tail broke off. A disc concealed at the back of the bomb now rose and pulled on chains attaching it to the main body of the bomb, which armed the device.

A large part of the bomb was devoted to buoyancy chambers, so after a brief period of rapid diving the bomb would rise back up to the surface and hit the underside of the ship, which had by this point presumably passed over it. Upon contact a 113-pound

HMS *Belfast* shortly after commissioning, reflecting the original state of the ship. Much would change over the next few decades. (Author's collection)

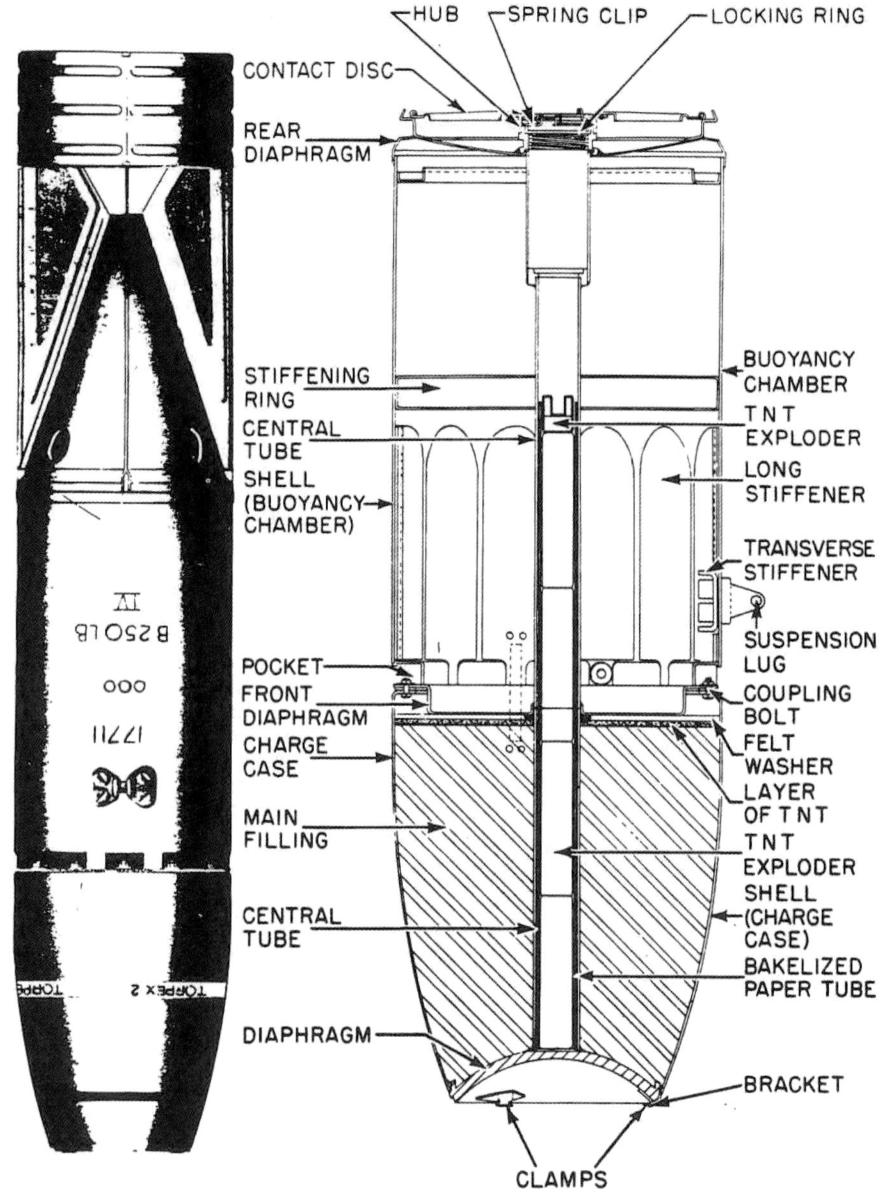

The B. 250lb. Mk IV (Service), or 'B Bomb,' is seen here showing both the unusual concave nose shape and the buoyancy chamber, which would in theory allow it to blow holes in the underside of enemy vessels, thus making it easier to sink ships by letting water in the bottom than air in the top. (*OP 1665, British Explosive Ordnance*, USN)

Torpex charge would detonate, punching a hole in the ship and bypassing most antitorpedo defences. Ideally the bomb would explode beneath a magazine or the machinery spaces. If it missed altogether, the bomb would eventually fill with water and sink once more.

Innovative as the idea was (and compared with early-war level bombing attempts on ships it could scarcely have done worse), the B bomb was apparently never used in combat, although development work on it continued until at least the middle of World War II. In any case, the development of the B Bomb showed how much attention was being paid to the effects of underwater explosions at the time.

The change from quadruple to triple turrets meant that the additional displacement that had been allocated to the heavier armament could in part be redirected to thicker armour. In previous Town-class ships the main belt along the sides of the hull had protected the machinery spaces and 4-inch magazines, while the 6-inch magazines had their own "box" armour, much like that of the earlier County-class heavy cruisers. This saved some weight but was less than ideal from an efficiency and overall protection perspective. Designers therefore proposed to extend the 4.5-inch main belt in a more conventional manner to cover the ship's vitals from the A turret magazine all the way back to the Y turret magazine. Deck armour would also be increased from 1.25 to 2 inches over the machinery spaces and from 2 to 3 inches over the magazines. At first it seemed that these changes would require too much displacement, and an odd hybrid layout putting the X and Y magazines behind the main belt and leaving A and B in their own boxes was developed; but with the relaxation of controls on final displacement, the original proposals were taken forward in full. The turrets were protected by up to 4 inches of armour on their faces, with additional protection over the steering gear, barbettes, and bridge area in varying thicknesses from splinter-proof up to 2 inches.

The ship's main armament consisted of 12 of the 6-inch Mk XXIII guns in a revised Mk XXIII turret (previous Town-class cruisers had used the Mk XXII turret). This "long trunk" design allowed shells and their charges to go directly from the ship's magazines to the turrets themselves, whereas in earlier "short trunk" turrets these went to a handling room below the turret, where they were transferred to another set of hoists and hand-ups to take them to the turret. In theory this change improved the rate of fire as well as requiring fewer crew.

The guns themselves could each elevate independently, which technically made them 3-gun turrets; but we shall use "triple" and other similar variants thereof to describe gun turrets for the sake of simplicity in this book. For a number of reasons the middle gun was set back slightly compared with those on either side. Designers hoped this placement would mitigate the blast effects of firing the guns, which could otherwise interfere with the flight path and thus accuracy of the shells; it also made better use of the turrets' internal space for the three gun crews and provided them more room to work; finally it also helped balance the turret to ensure the ship didn't list when the main guns were trained to port or starboard. However, the guns had to be loaded at a maximum of 12.5 degrees elevation, otherwise the breech would hit the gun well that allowed the weapon to elevate up to 45 degrees for firing. In theory that could slow the ship's rate of fire at longer ranges, although in practice very few long-range engagements by large warships ever approached the theoretical maximum rate of fire. The two aft turrets were also elevated by one deck level compared with the older Town-class variants, placing them on the same levels as the corresponding forward turrets.

John Harrison (petty officer ordnance artificer [OA] for A and B turrets in Belfast in the early part of World War II):

When you're passing out on [gunnery training] one of the tests is, you're taken on a ship and you do a gun test. Now this gun test comprises of a battery of

HMS *Birmingham*, *Belfast*'s half-sister, illustrates the lower aft turrets, split hangar, and more forward funnel location of the Town class. (Author's collection)

Belfast moored at Hong Kong toward the end of World War II. This view affords a good look at the guns she mounted during this period. (Public domain)

*6-inch guns on a ship and you have to offset the sights. You're given the range of the target-towing ship and you're given the offset, and you offset the sights so that the gun layer is looking at the target-towing ship, but the shells are to hit the target being towed some 200 yards behind. You are then taken on board the target-towing ship and the signal was given for the firing. You're all watching the target; splash, splash, splash on one side and over the side of this target-towing ship another two splashes. Somebody hadn't offset their target telling sights! Big signals went flashing, but of course by that time there were two more on the way over, accompanied by the other four on the target being towed. Anyway, when we got back on board, there was big reprimand of one of the OAs and it didn't go any further. Years and years later I was diving down at Weymouth and I mentioned this to an ex-Navy chap. And he said "I was on a ****** ship target towing, and it's on the bottom of Weymouth Bay at the moment. These things came over, went down the engine hatch, and knocked a plate out, and we turned over and sank later; it's somewhere out there." He said it's not the first time it happened.*

The secondary battery was improved over the previous Town class. The same dual-purpose (DP) Mk XVI* 4-inch gun was used in the Mk XIX twin mounting, but there were now 6 of them, 3 per side, for a total of 12 guns as opposed to the 4 mounts used on *Belfast*'s smaller predecessors.

The dedicated antiaircraft (AA) suite was also improved. Again the same weapon was utilized, in this case the 2-pounder (40-mm) pom-pom, but this time a pair of octuple mountings instead of the previous ships' quadruple mountings were installed. This was supplemented to questionable effect by a pair of quadruple .50-calibre Vickers machine gun mounts and pintle mounts for five twin .303-inch Lewis guns.

Denis Watkinson (served on board Belfast *in the later stages of World War II):*

You know you have a pretty wide gap (between shell hoist and 4-inch gun). There's your guns alongside the ship, and here is your conveyor belt and the shells are coming up this end and you pick them off there. Couple of steps and then you're putting it into the gun. That was one of my jobs when I first went on to the Belfast*, after that I was the trainer. I used to train the guns, which is a different job. You'd have to be pretty fit, because the 4-inch shell is about two foot, the actual shell part, and then you've got the brass charge. Honestly, if you got a proper routine, you know you take the cover off and there's a rack here with little wheels on, now you shove that up the boat and there's a captain of the gun standing there and the other ones (of the gun crew) putting shells into the other gun.*

The final element of the ship's main armament consisted of two triple Mk IV* torpedo launchers, one located on each side of the ship, carrying some variation of the 21-inch Mk IX torpedo depending on the year. These were provided mainly for use against other cruisers and larger warships should *Belfast* run into them.

The ship was also equipped with Asdic (now known as sonar) to assist with antisubmarine capabilities, along with depth charge rails, although the initial load of just six depth charges spoke to the fact that this was very much viewed as a last-ditch emergency capability.

GUNS OF HMS *BELFAST*

Belfast was equipped with a main battery, a secondary/AA battery, and a dedicated AA battery.

Main Battery: 6-inch/50 BL Mark XXIII

A new gun was developed in the early 1930s after the London Naval Treaty created the light cruiser armed with a maximum gun calibre of 6.1 inches. The last 6-inch gun had been designed a decade earlier for use on capital ships. Originally the Mark XXIV version was planned for the ship in the quadruple turret setup, although that failed to progress to the final design stages.

Secondary/AA Battery: 4-inch/45 QF Mark XIX

The Mark XIX was a popular and near-universal AA gun on British cruisers and destroyers. On *Belfast* the battery was fed by a long conveyor system because the magazines and thus hoists were some distance forward.

Dedicated AA Battery: 2-pound QF Mark VIII Pom-Pom

Available in single, quadruple, and octuple mountings, the pom-poms saw continued improvement through their service lives but were always a little inferior to the 40-mm Bofors in terms of range. However, the long belt feeds gave them unprecedented continuous firing time, which could be extended on multiple gun mounts by firing half the guns and then switching to the other half once the belt ran out to allow the first half to be reloaded. This proved especially useful against kamikazes later in the war.

While *Belfast* turned out to be the last of the "full size" British light cruisers (the *Fiji*/Crown Colony–

The interior of one of *Belfast*'s remaining 4-inch/45 twin mountings. Most of the guns on the ship today are from different manufacturers and different years, even in the same mount, illustrating the wartime need to get any working gun onto the ship when an old one was worn out. (Author's collection)

class ships then under construction were attempts to fit the original Town-class armament into a smaller hull as per the Second London Treaty, an agreement that was voided by withdrawal and violation almost before the ink was dry), this was largely because World War II broke out. Suggestions for an "Improved *Belfast*" cropped up a number of times during the early and middle parts of World War II, but budget and material constraints led to the idea being dropped before light cruiser design eventually morphed into the distinctly different *Neptune* and *Minotaur* concepts.

TABLE 3.1. MAIN BATTERY

Training speed:	7 degrees per second
Elevation rate:	10 degrees per second
Maximum elevation:	45 degrees
Firing cycle:	7.5–10 seconds
Ammunition carried:	200 rounds/gun (not including practice rounds)
Shell weight (pounds/kilograms):	112/50.8
Muzzle velocity (feet per second/ meters per second):	2,758/841
Maximum range (yards/meters):	25,480/23,300

3.2. SECONDARY/AA BATTERY

Training speed:	15–20 degrees per second once converted to powered mounts
Elevation rate:	15–20 degrees per second once converted to powered mounts
Maximum elevation:	80 degrees
Firing cycle:	3–4 seconds
Ammunition carried:	250 rounds/gun (not including practice rounds)
Shell weight (pounds/kilograms):	66.75/30.3
Muzzle velocity (feet per second/ meters per second):	2,660/811
Maximum range (yards/meters):	19,850/18,150

3.3. DEDICATED AA BATTERY

Training speed:	15 degrees per second, 25 when powered
Elevation rate:	15 degrees per second, 25 when powered
Maximum elevation:	80 degrees
Firing cycle:	0.6 seconds
Ammunition carried:	2,500 rounds/gun
Shell weight (pounds/kilograms):	2/0.91
Muzzle velocity (feet per second/ meters per second):	2,400/732
Maximum range (yards/meters):	5,000/4,572

Shown here are the general layout of the *Minotaur* and *Neptune* concepts contrasted with that of *Belfast* in her World War II guise. *Neptune* was considerably larger to support fast-loading, dual-purpose 6-inch guns in triple turrets, which imposed a considerable weight penalty. *Minotaur* used twin turrets instead to try to reduce complexity and weight. Neither design was constructed, although the turret design for the *Minotaur* was later adapted to become the *Tiger*-class cruisers' main battery. (Ship models from World of Warships, arranged by Ryan P)

INTO SERVICE

Belfast's launching, 17 months prior to her commissioning and only 18 months prior to the outbreak of World War II. (Imperial War Museum)

The contract to build *Belfast* was issued to Harland and Wolff—fittingly a yard in the ship's namesake city—on 10 September 1936, and the keel was laid exactly three months later. The hull was launched on 17 March 1938, before fitting out, and sea trials saw her commissioned on 3 August 1939—a total of 31 months and 24 days after her keel was laid.

John Harrison:

Then there was a new ship we'd heard of being built in Ireland called HMS Belfast*. And I got an admiral's inspection, I came out with all credits on that, and they said, "Right, you're on draught." I said, where am I going to? "HMS* Belfast*."*

Belfast's first assignment was to the Second Cruiser Squadron, part of the Home Fleet, alongside *Southampton* and *Glasgow*. Her first (and as it turned out only) peacetime mission was as the protagonist of Operation Hipper, wherein she played the role of the German cruiser *Admiral Hipper* and tried to get from the North Sea into the Atlantic to conduct commerce raiding while evading the Home Fleet's patrols.

The operation, which began on 14 August, was a success for the brand-new ship. Capt. George Arthur Scott took *Belfast* through the Pentland Firth, the narrow and dangerous passage between the Orkney Islands and mainland Scotland, at night, thus evading the rest of the Home Fleet and pointing out a weakness in British patrol routines that could now be remedied before a real enemy exploited it.

The ship's aircraft catapult had not yet been completed, although she had sailed with all the requisite parts, and she was on her way down to Portsmouth at the conclusion of the exercise to put them all together when new orders came through. War with Germany was expected to begin any day, and the ship was to be part of the 18th Cruiser Squadron, comprising the smaller *Aurora*, *Belfast*'s sister ship *Edinburgh*, and their relative *Sheffield*. So the ship had to turn around and head for her base at Scapa Flow. The declaration of war on 3 September 1939 found the squadron at sea with their first mission: to form part of the naval blockade of Germany. The Royal Navy had conducted a similar mission over the course of World War I, and it was hoped that the results would be similar: a slowly tightening noose around Germany's economic effort.

John Harrison:

We headed south and were getting really excited to get back to the girlfriends etc. We were off I suppose the entrance to the Thames Estuary and I was writing a letter and the sun was straining through the porthole, shining on the deck, and suddenly this spot of light moved and it moved away and disappeared. I thought, well, wait a minute, that shouldn't happen, the sun doesn't move like that, we must be. . . . I looked out and looked over the side and there was a big arch of where our wake had gone. We were heading north again.

Almost a week later, on 8 September, *Belfast* and her sister joined the battlecruisers *Hood* and *Renown* along with a destroyer escort for a more aggressive sweep. They were looking specifically for enemy raiders, both warships and converted merchantmen, but found nothing over the subsequent two weeks of searching. Indeed, the first of the German raiders had already sailed and positioned themselves far out in the oceans.

Farther south, HMS *Spearfish*, an S-class submarine, had been probing German defences when she was attacked by German warships. Although she survived, it was quickly discovered that she was unable to dive again after the commander brought her to the surface to assess the damage. In an operation that illustrates just how early in the war this was, a huge task force was assembled that included the carrier HMS *Ark Royal*, the battleship *Nelson*, the battlecruiser *Hood*, and numerous cruisers and destroyers—all to rescue one small submarine. Despite the best efforts of numerous Luftwaffe Ju-88s, the rescue effort was successful. A single 550-pound bomb hit on *Hood* inflicted minor damage, while *Belfast* herself was treated to an interesting display of waterspouts but little else.

October rolled around, and *Belfast* finally got the chance to interact with enemy surface shipping while on blockade patrol duty. The weather had improved, making both spotting the enemy and then boarding easier; at this point *Belfast* did not yet possess any radar that could have been of use in tracking enemy shipping. On the ninth, just before 0900, a ship was spotted in the distance. After about a quarter of an hour the vessel was identified as SS *Tai Yin*, a Norwegian-owned merchantman that was nonetheless considered suspicious. After another half hour the two ships were close enough for a boarding party to inspect the cargo ship, and just after 1100 a prize crew was ordered to take her to the United Kingdom for further inspection. Barely a couple of minutes later another vessel was spotted. This ship initially identified herself as SS *Ancona*, a neutral Swedish vessel, but it became quickly apparent that she was in fact the German liner SS *Cap Norte* in the process of trying to get back to Germany. *Belfast* sent over a significantly stronger armed boarding party, which arrived just in time to stop the crew from scuttling the liner. When it became evident that there were German army reservists amongst the passengers, another prize crew was sent over and *Cap Norte* also began making tracks for Scotland. Three days later, on

Belfast **in October 1939 shortly after the start of World War II. This is one of very few photos of the ship in her originally commissioned state. (Imperial War Museum)**

the twelfth, yet another ship was spotted, boarded, and sent on under a prize crew for inspection. This ship was *Uddeholm* and was genuinely Swedish. With her complement somewhat depleted from having had to provide three prize crews, *Belfast* also set sail for home to recover her crew as well as to refuel and conduct minor repairs.

John Harrison:

Later there was a big merchant ship coming down flying the German flag and we had instructions to board. She was full of German diplomats coming back to Germany; she was called the Cap Norte. And we sent a boarding party aboard there, and they escorted this Cap Norte to Scapa Flow. This was the Saturday when war was declared on the Sunday, somebody must have known an awful lot for us to do a thing like that. It was a little bit cold because when we were due to go back to port, we were due to get the rest of the Arctic gear. All we had on board [was] summer gear. One learns an awful lot about self-protection, like you do not have a hot water shave. If there's liable to be action stations because as soon as you dash out you get frostbite on your soft skin and it's most painful.

With most of the fleet out at sea, *Belfast* and other ships of the 18th Cruiser Squadron found plenty of room to select an anchorage in Scapa Flow. In the distance HMS *Royal Oak*, the most modernized of the *Revenge*-class battleships, was peacefully swinging at anchor. The night of 13–14 October changed all that. The peace ended as the battleship was subjected to repeated attacks from *U-47*, which had penetrated the somewhat patchy antisubmarine defences and launched a series of torpedoes that sent *Royal Oak* to the bottom with the loss of 835 men. The following morning *Belfast* and many of the other ships still present were ordered to the backup anchorage of Ault Bea in Lock Ewe.

Fearing that the success of *U-47*'s raid had emboldened the Kriegsmarine, the Royal Navy put together a force consisting of *Nelson*, *Rodney*, *Hood*, and the carrier *Furious* along with a destroyer flotilla and the cruiser *Aurora*, to which *Belfast* was also added. This powerful fleet patrolled as a backstop to the line of armed merchant cruisers just in case anything especially interesting came up out of the North Sea.

But no German warships appeared. At the end of the month, on 25 October, *Belfast* went into dock at Govan, then headed out on 7 November to a new assignment with her old formation, the Second Cruiser Squadron. Alongside *Southampton*, *Glasgow*, and *Aurora*, she found herself in company with the older cruiser *Enterprise* and ten of the latest destroyers, all based at Rosyth. Together they formed a fast striking force that could respond to any emerging German threat at sea except for potentially *Scharnhorst*—although the general opinion on board seemed to be that the formation could take on that behemoth as well!

STRIKING A MINE

On 21 November the strike force was ordered to sea. It would be *Belfast*'s last assignment for some years. She, *Southampton*, and two destroyers were to conduct gunnery exercises on their way out of the anchorage. By 0947 the ship was past the harbour's antisubmarine defences. Heading out to sea meant a well-understood danger from mines. German aircraft had been seen dropping parachute mines in British waters since shortly after the war began, and there were sure to be many submarine- or ship-laid mines that had been deployed unseen as well. For safety's sake the ship ran out the paravanes—small, winged, torpedo-shaped devices. One was attached on either side of the ship with a strong steel cable, which was supposed to cut the mooring line of any mine it came across. The mine would then float to the surface, where it could be spotted and destroyed with gunfire. The vast majority of ship–mine encounters occurred when the currents formed by a ship moving through the water "sucked in" a mine floating just to port or starboard, which made the paravane defence a viable one against moored contact-detonation mines; head-on collisions were very rare.

But despite these measures, at 1052, while steaming at 18 knots, the ship was rocked by a violent explosion. She immediately lost way and slowed to a stop. Initially those on board thought the explosion was the result of a torpedo hit. The ship's boats were swung out in case the damage was fatal, and damage control parties moved quickly to secure the ship and work out the extent of the damage.

John Harrison:

Southampton *was the flagship run at Rosyth; we were ordered to sea behind the* Southampton *and we had destroyers out. Now the* Southampton *steamed underneath the Forth Bridge and then signaled that she was returning to base. It appeared that there was a seaman on board who got appendicitis, which had gone very bad, and the surgeon on board said, "Get this man back to hospital, I'll operate ashore." She [*Southampton*] returned to Rosyth, we then became lead ship.* Belfast *was steaming along on a glorious day and standees was piped, which means that everybody who wasn't on duty was on the upper deck. I was on duty (in one of the forward turrets) charging these 3,000-pound air bottles (that allowed the guns to elevate) with two qualified ordnance men and I was standing over the 20-foot ladder going down to the shell room listening to the noises the bottles made, not a lot.*

The extent of the mine damage is visible on the ship in drydock. Most ships this badly damaged would have been scrapped. (Imperial War Museum)

In the immediate aftermath of the mining, the crew prepared the ship's boats in case the damage proved fatal. (Imperial War Museum)

The air pressure was coming up and suddenly I felt a terrific thud and I felt my spine going into my skull and everything went dark. My original thought was "the air bottles have exploded" but then I thought "I can't be thinking about an air bottle if I'm dead." Then the dead silence, followed by a shaking up and down as though you were shaking a doll up and down, then it went very quiet and I was still standing over this hole leading to the shell room. "Well," I said to the others, "we'd better try and get out of here." Now, the only way you can get out of a working space is through a little S-bend and up through this little hatch between the right-hand gun and the centre gun, which you can still see, that's the only way out.

Tried to force that up and water came in. Now in virtual pitch black you think, "Right? We're sunk." Anyway, we managed to get this thing open and the water was from the drenching gear that had been distorted by the force of the explosion and was facing straight down this hatch, much to our relief. We got out and assessed the damage. The damage had been reported by the time we got out as it was quite a lengthy time. The destroyer escort said, "Your keel is hanging off now."

If you see the size of the Belfast*, can you realise that the power of that explosion had bent or lifted the forward part of the ship from the catapult upward 22 foot at least out of the water? Cause we were 18 foot draught and it needed to be 22 foot out of water so a destroyer escort could see the keel hanging off. It is remarkable but that did happen. They could have made a mistake or been joking, I thought, but when we managed to get back into the dry dock or into the dock in Rosyth, they started to let the water out. They let six foot of water out of the forward part of the ship. A turret and B turret had dropped some eight to ten foot, proving that our keel was in fact missing. That is the power of the explosion of a magnetic mine. Now the magnetic mines were not really known about at the time, it was just a big mine. Now it turned out that that mine had been laid by a submarine.*

In fact the ship had been hit by a magnetic-influence mine, a type of antiship weapon that could be set far deeper than a normal mine and was thus immune to paravane sweeps. The mine detonated when a significant interference in the local magnetic field—such as several thousand tons of ferrous metal passing overhead—passed close enough to trip the fuse. Additionally, unlike a contact mine, the explosion itself did not deal much damage directly to its target. In ideal conditions (for the mine) the shock wave and a rising bubble of gas lifts the affected vessel amidships, breaking its keel and twisting its structure. This is exacerbated when the gas bubble vents out into the air and the ship's centre falls back into a temporary void, crushing already weakened structural elements. To add final insult to injury, the collapsing gas bubble is followed by an upwelling jet of water that can break the weakened ship in two.

Numerous factors can affect the damage such a mine actually does, including the size of the explosive, the depth of the mine, the size of the ship relative to the first two factors, and so on. In this case, the effect was not enough to cause fatal damage, but the ship was still crippled.

1112
To: D Four
From: Belfast
Please keep me informed of your condition so that I can inform C-in-C Rosyth

1115
To: D Four
From: Belfast
Keep Destroyers on the move screening me

1114
To: Belfast
From: D Four
Do you require towing?

1115
From: Belfast
Yes certainly

1116
From: Belfast
"A" Boiler and Engine Room out of action. Improbable that steam can be raised. Explosion was abreast A Boiler Room

To: Belfast
From: Euryalus
Can we be of any assistance? Divers are dressed and all ready

1125
To: Euryalus
From: Belfast
Return to harbour and be ready to help when we return to harbour

To: Belfast
From: Whitley
Shall I come alongside your starboard side forward to facilitate passing tow

1130
To: D Four, Whitley
From: Belfast
Tug Krooman *is endeavouring to tow me if he is able to do so, keep* Whitley *screening*

1131
To: Whitley
From: Belfast
Keep on the move

1133
To: Krooman
From: Belfast
Come alongside starboard bow, slip your targets

1137
To: Belfast
From: Euryalus
Shall I take the target from Tug?

From: Belfast
Yes tug has slipped target endeavour to get them in tow

1148
To: D Four
From: Belfast
Report to Rosyth that Tug Krooman *is towing, but further assistance is urgently required. Ship will not be able to steam and probably not steer. Approximate casualties Dead NIL Injured 16*

1211
To: Belfast
From: D Four
Is it certain that it was a torpedo please?

1216
To: D Four
From: Belfast
No I cannot tell as nothing was seen

1249
To: Belfast *for CD*
From: AS
Outer caisson of lock is open. Ship can enter lock whenever there is sufficient depth of water to navigate main channel

Belfast **under tow and heading back to harbour after the flooding was stabilised, as seen from a supporting ship. (Imperial War Museum)**

1259
To: C-in-C Rosyth, CS2. CD
From: Belfast
Explosion at about 80 and possibly two other right aft. Ship flooded to waterline from 66 to 93.4 in. HA magazine flooded. Making water in forward Engine Room and possibly "A" Boiler Room. Steam cannot be raised except for one dynamo as all Turbo oil fuel pumps out of action. Steering gear in use. Draught increased to two feet forward to four inches aft. Oil fuel cannot be pumped out forward. Casualties; Dead NIL. 21 injured, some seriously. Hope to arrive for immediate docking 1500, essential to dry dock immediately.

1303
To: AS
From: CD
Propose to berth Belfast *in "Y" berth. Will you please clear berth, rough time of arrival 1630 today Tuesday.*

1313
To: D Four
From: Belfast
Destroyers are to continue screening up to the Gate so far as navigationally possible and to remain in close company till ship enters basin.

1349
To: Belfast
From: D Four
C-in-C and RAD think I am hunting. May I take Gurkha *and* Isis *and search when you have reached Inchkeith.*

1351
To: D Four
From: Belfast
Yes I had no idea that you were supposed to be hunting. Many thanks for your screening.

1400
To: CD
From: Belfast
At 1315 draught was as follows: 23 feet 9 forward 22 feet aft

The tug assigned to tow the targets for the now abandoned gunnery exercise made her way over and less than an hour after the explosion had *Belfast* under tow. A couple of hours later, three more tugs sent out from Rosyth turned up to share the load. By 1700 that afternoon *Belfast* was back in the dockyard offloading casualties as destroyers hovered nearby, partially in case something ruptured or exploded inside the ship and partially in case an enemy had followed them back through the Gate. With this task complete, the ship proceeded into drydock at 2230 ready for a survey the following day once the dock was pumped out. But this task had to be suspended when it became evident that the dramatic distortion in *Belfast*'s upper deck reflected something far more concerning deeper inside the ship. Placed on keel blocks designed for a normal ship, *Belfast* was not sitting evenly and was crushing the few blocks she was resting on. Divers sent down reported the keel was hogged, or bent upward, from just under B turret all the way to just behind the aft funnel, with the worst deflection being just under the ship's hangar.

John Harrison:

> *Now, over the radio a man called Lord Haw Haw from Germany had announced that HMS* Belfast *had been sunk with heavy loss of life. Well, no. We knew that was a load of codswallop because about a week before he'd said that HMS* Excellent, *Whale Island, had been also sunk with heavy, heavy loss of life (and the fact I'd just got off the ship). We in the Navy knew that, but the civvies didn't. So I thought, well, I'll ring my wife from the little phone box at the top end of Inverkeithing. And the conversation went like this. "Ohh hello* Norfolk.*"*
>
> *And the (operator's) voice said, "Where are you speaking from?"*
>
> *I said, "Inverkeithing."*
>
> *"Can you alphabetically spell that?"*
>
> *Can you imagine with a box of matches in darkness, striking matches to spell out Inverkeithing to him? The voice said, "OK Inverkeithing, right, you're through."*
>
> *And I spoke to my wife, she said, "So the* Belfast's *been sunk with heavy loss of life?"*
>
> *"It's actually in dock."*
>
> *Great relief anyway.*

Steps having been taken to ensure that no more water would enter the ship, the drydock was reflooded and the ship was taken out to be lightened while spare softwood blocks were cut to the new shape of the keel to properly support it. The single most visible evidence of the lightening process was the removal of the main battery, including the turrets, which as it turned out had jumped off their roller paths as a result of the explosion and would have had to be removed for repair and reseating anyway. With *Belfast* back in the drydock a more extensive survey could begin. The reading was grim. The damage included but was not limited to:

- Unseating of the four main battery turrets and associated damage to the roller bearings
- Partial collapse of the foremast top
- All antiaircraft directors damaged and out of action

A close-up view of the damage to *Belfast* on the port side (opposite the mine strike) shows how the full width of the hull was distorted. (Imperial War Museum)

- Four of the six twin 4-inch guns out of action (the aftmost pair remained operational)
- Starboard torpedo launchers out of action after being knocked off their roller path
- Hull fractures extending from keel to the upper deck
- Fractured mountings on all turbines bar one aft
- Fuel pipes fractured and leaking
- Forward port turbine gear case fractured
- General damage to various electrical equipment
- Approximately half of the auxiliary machinery crippled
- Severe buckling of the hull from keel to the armour belt directly under the forward rangefinder
- Bow dropped about two feet off line
- Deck plating, structural pillar, and hull fracturing immediately aft of the hangar in the vicinity of the 4-inch magazine
- General deck, bulkhead, and keel buckling along the length previously described

In most circumstances a ship damaged so extensively would probably have been scrapped—had she made it back to port at all—but *Belfast* had three advantages. (1) It was early days in the war, and even extensive repairs might still bring her back into useful operation before the war's end. (2) Being an almost new ship, her loss would be far more keenly felt than a C- or *Leander*-class cruiser in the same circumstance. (3) The changes made to the design of *Belfast* and *Edinburgh* had mitigated the impact of the damage somewhat.

The last was more critical than is sometimes appreciated. Although the alterations in the placement of her machinery had not prevented the loss of propulsion after the explosion, they had probably saved the ship. The immediate uncontrolled flooding caused by the hull breach had filled various storerooms and then spread though the forward emergency steering position and a number of other similarly small compartments. However, if one overlays the layout of a conventional Town-class cruiser atop that of *Belfast*, it is immediately apparent that the immediate flooding in an older ship would have been in the forward boiler rooms, with much of the significant fracturing occurring in the vicinity of the forward engine spaces. This much larger volume of space being flooded would have caused considerably greater peril to the ship as well as exerting significant stress immediately forward of the aforementioned fractures, which themselves would be in an area with significantly less internal structure. While it is impossible to say with certainty, it is quite possible that a conventional Town class might well have foundered or broken in two when subjected to a similar detonation; at the very least, recovery of the ship would have been far more fraught.

Despite the initial pessimism, *Belfast* would sail again after an extensive refit and with a mostly new crew. (Imperial War Museum)

Final Report of circumstances attending to the explosion on HMS BELFAST

Sir,

1. I have the honour to forward the accompanying final report in connection with the explosion which occurred in H M Ship under my command on November 21, 1939.
2. HMS BELFAST sailed from Rosyth at 0917 on Tuesday November 21, in company with the Vice-Admiral Commanding the Second Cruiser Squadron in the *Southampton*, and two destroyers, to carry out an exercise programme in the Firth of Forth.
3. At 1030 the *Southampton* was about to carry out a sub-calibre practice, and at this time the *Belfast* was 4 cables astern of her; course 025 degrees, speed 17 knots.
4. At 1037 course was altered together to 295 degrees, at 1042 to 115 degrees, and at 1049 to 060 degrees.
5. The rudder had just been put amidships at the conclusion of the last alteration of course—the ship's head at the time being about 065 degrees—when, at 1052, a violent explosion occurred, apparently under the foremast. At this time, the *Southampton* bore 030 degrees, approximately 4.5 cables.
6. The order "Stop Both" was given, and subsequently "Half-ahead Both"—"Hard-a-Starboard." The ship answered the rudder until she lost steerage way and was put on a course for Inchkeith, but the main engines were out of action from the moment of the explosion.
7. The tracks of both ships are shown from 1035 in Enclosure I on a scale of 1 inch to 1,000 yards.
8. The explosion occurred in position 56° 06′ 49″ N, 2° 54′ 36″ W, in approximately 18 fathoms of water. Little or no tidal stream was running at the time; this position was about 4 cables to the Eastward of the original line of advance of 025 degrees.
9. The weather was calm.
10. The maximum number of lookouts were closed up at the time, and no track of torpedo or discharge bursts was observed; opinions vary as to the number of explosions. Officers situated forward felt one explosion. Some of those aft considered there was more than one explosion, and two columns of water. A large column of water and smoke came up abreast the mainmast starboard side.
11. All doors, valves etc., not already shut, were promptly closed, and preparations were made to be taken in tow. The fresh water system was switched off; and such floats and rafts as were available were prepared for lowering over the side if required.
12. A number of destroyers and escort vessels closed immediately after the explosion, and I ordered them to keep on the move screening round the BELFAST.
13. In the meantime every endeavour was being made to ascertain the nature of the damage to the ship, and at 1116 a signal was made to the Commander-in-Chief, Rosyth, to the effect that it was improbable that steam could be raised (vide Enclosure II).
14. By 1133 the Tug *Krooman* had closed to within a cable of the BELFAST, and she was ordered to slip the targets which she had been towing, and to take the BELFAST in tow. Shortly after 1140 she commenced to tow, and the ship began to move slowly in the direction of Inchkeith. HMS BELFAST'S steering gear continued to work normally throughout the operation.
15. At 1148 a further signal was made to Rosyth with the information that the *Krooman* was towing, but that more assistance was urgently required, and at 1259 a more comprehensive signal giving the known states of the ship and addition that it was essential to drydock immediately, was sent to the Commander-in-Chief, Rosyth.

16. At 1302 the Tug *Brahman* arrived from Rosyth and commenced to tow from forward with the *Krooman* and between 1314 and 1333 the tugs *Grangebourne*, *Oxcar*, and *Bulger* arrived and were secured on port and starboard quarters and on the starboard side amidships respectively.

17. From the moment of the *Brahman*'s arrival HMS BELFAST continued to make good progress and Inchkeith was passed at 1411 and the Gate at 1520. At 1700 the BELFAST was secured in the lock in Rosyth dockyard, and the work of landing the casualties commenced (vide Appendix IV).

18. The handling of all tugs was good throughout, the operation of taking the BELFAST into the lock, conducted by the Tug *Brahman*, being particularly well carried out.

19. HMS BELFAST was subsequently moved and secured in dry dock at 2230.

20. In view of the large alterations of course immediately prior to the explosion, and the fact that nothing was seen although a number of His Majesty's Ships were in the vicinity, I consider it most unlikely that the damage was caused by submarine attack. In my opinion, the BELFAST struck a mine; possibly more than one, though I do not think this was so.

21. The conduct of all officers and men was beyond praise; there was a complete absence of panic and all work was carried out in a quiet and normal manner. I have, in Appendix X, submitted to you the name of one rating who in my opinion is particularly deserving of your favourable consideration. Furthermore, I desire to draw your especial notice to Commander James Gregson Roper, Royal Navy, my executive officer. I cannot speak too highly of his work as Commander of the ship his abilities and untiring devotion to duty have, in my judgement, had their reward in that the personnel whom he has trained and the organisation which he has perfected, have reacted in sudden strain and emergency in accordance with the highest traditions of His Majesty's Service.

22. I therefore desire to submit to your special notice the following: COMMANDER JAMES GREGSON ROPER, ROYAL NAVY.

I have the honour to be
Sir,
Your obedient servant
(Signed) G. A. SCOTT
CAPTAIN, ROYAL NAVY

But even after she made it back to drydock *Belfast*'s survival was still a close-run thing. Only the vociferous insistence of some of the dockyard staff that she could be saved seems to have tipped the balance. Rosyth was not capable of the extensive rebuild that would be needed to get her back to sea, but *Belfast* was also not capable of moving under her own power. Extensive temporary repairs would have to be undertaken first, including reseating and realigning the engines and patching over the cracks in the hull. With it being clear that the process of getting the *Belfast* back into service would take years, she was paid off and decommissioned, and her valuable trained crew was distributed to other ships.

John Harrison:

You had a week's survivors leave, then you came back and all the crew who were not held back to assess the damage, I was, in A turret were drafted to HMS Hood*. That's why at the last count, there were only 15, maybe 20 people of the original crew that was still alive after the* Hood *blew up. At today's date [recording made in 2005], there's only four of us left. . . .*

Did I think she would ever go to sea again?

Never, no. The thing I remember was that the whole of the electrical equipment apart from the standby was out, fridges were dead, the stench inside that ship. . . . She was unstable. You could feel it as you moved about in the dock, you could feel she was unstable. I mean, the experience I had in that turret I knew something was happening and we thought well, this is it, but it appeared what they were going to do was to empty it as far as they could and float it on barrels to some shipyard to get it rebuilt, which is exactly what did happen.

It was floated round to all places in Devonport, and virtually every part of it was rebuilt. We had been so pleased that she was an all welded ship; now if she hadn't been all welded, when this happened the rivets would have sheared, in fact some of the rivets on the upper deck did shear. If she'd been conventionally built with rivets, they'd have sheared, and we'd have gone down and actually died. Other ships which have been mined and been riveted sank, but we had no rivets and that welding distorted, and when she was rebuilt they had great difficulty in welding extra strength where they'd broken. It's called puddle welding and they had great difficulty in welding that after the damage had taken place, during the straightening out. And that's why you've got extra strengthening where the catapult was on the Belfast *as she stands now, because the* Belfast *had this aircraft on a catapult going across the ship. Now if you want to design something with a crackability point, you'd do exactly what that catapult did, it had a crack across it.*

It was late June when she finally sailed from Rosyth, proceeding south along the east coast of Scotland, then England, into the Channel, and finally to Devonport, arriving after a three-day voyage arranged in secret to deny the German coastal batteries and attack craft near the Strait of Dover a chance to have a go at her.

One of the first lessons from both *Belfast*'s damage and damage received by other Town-class ships early in the war was that the forecastle break represented a stress point where stress from impacts accumulated and caused structural failures. This would be addressed in her reconstruction, but the lessons would also be applied to other ships of the class as they came in for refits.

Belfast would be out of action for a while. By the time she reemerged into active service all the Town class that would be lost during the war had been sunk: *Southampton*, *Gloucester*, her sister ship *Edinburgh*, and finally *Manchester*. Lessons from their loss plus damage to other ships would be incorporated into *Belfast*'s own repairs.

The strength of the ship's repairs would soon be tested in the rough seas on Arctic convoy protection duty. (Imperial War Museum)

RESTORATION

Contrast the following page with the ship's previous profile, seen here entering Belfast Harbour during her first commission. (Imperial War Museum)

The process of bringing *Belfast* back into action was slowed somewhat by two main factors. First, much of her removable material, with the exception of the main machinery and the 6-inch battery, was "acquired" by other ships to keep them in action; thus, new replacements had to be ordered and constructed.

Second, the Luftwaffe had been tasked with hampering the operations of the Royal Dockyards, and they did a very good job of it. Devonport's position on the south coast of England made it a relatively easy target for bombing raids that disrupted transport of supplies and work schedules. Warehouses were hit and workers dived for cover on a routine basis.

Nonetheless, after stores and most of the main machinery were removed, the ship was carefully placed onto blocks. The blocks were adjusted similarly to those in Rosyth but with even more precise care, because the ship had to be positioned on as close to an even keel as possible in order to determine the precise extent of the hull's deformation. The original plans and the full-scale drawings expanded from them, made at the shipyard where she was built, were acquired and compared with precise measurements of her current state. These comparisons revealed the exact nature and extent of the deformation, including the fact that at the point of greatest deformation, at frame 80 just under the ship's hangar, the entire hull followed the bend in the keel. That meant the entire hull would have to be adjusted as opposed to simply cutting out and replacing individual components.

This procedure involved a complex ballet requiring considerable skill. The hull was shored up with additional blocks and braces, the blocks capped by greased wedges to allow for easy adjustment. A significant portion of the ship from beneath the bridge to the back of the forward machinery spaces was also heavily shored up internally.

Once the hull was stabilized, the dockyard workers started at the fore and aftmost areas of distortion and began removing the main support blocks. The unsupported hull then began to settle under its own weight, bending back toward true, with the adjustable wedges of the newly installed side-blocks used to control the rate of descent. This process ran 24/7 for 16 days in a time before laser rangefinders and other sophisticated devices were available. Instead, dozens of men swarmed over the slowly settling ship with tape measures, rulers, theodolites, and other equipment as 10,000 tons of steel gradually lowered itself above them. In the worst affected area, immediately beneath and aft of the hangar, the upper portion of the ship refused to settle. Huge water tanks were placed atop the ship in this area and then filled to force the ship down, but even this had no success. Given that this area was where the hull had fractured as well as bent, the dockyard managers concluded the section was permanently distorted, and the hull structure had to be removed and replaced. Once that was accomplished, the machinery was reinstalled and the superstructure, which had been removed, was reconstructed. Any remaining slight variation to the line of the keel should, it was hoped, sort itself out once all the ship's equipment was back on board and the hull began flexing as it proceeded at speed through the sea once more, albeit that would be some time in the future.

John Harrison:

The damage to the turrets, now we're talking about 500 ton of turret, the explosion was so violent as to lift that forward part of the ship and break it because the bell was broken, the keel was broken, and it had lifted that turret up. Now, the clamps holding the revolving part of the turret to the fixed part of the turret are U clamps. They're shaped like a U and they are one inch thick. When I crept round the edge, you can still see into the depth below the deck and the gun turret body itself, that is where all the communications go around and you can actually creep down around that. I crept round there and measured the gap in some of these U-clips, which should have been quarter of an inch, and some of them were an inch as they'd been straightened out with the force that lifted that gun turret up with its three huge guns.

Fixing and assessing this took some time, as the ship's crew was gradually breaking up. And I can assure you, round there with a little torch, hearing the creaking and groaning of a turret gradually sagging, you've got to live that. I got out and made my report and the ship was very vacant because there was nobody there except us few.

Thomas Miles, W. H. Allen & Sons and Company Ltd.:

Two days after the vessel had been damaged and she was in dry dock in Rosyth, I accompanied Mr. Dalton, chief electrical draughtsman. I was asked to report on the damage to the electrical gear of our manufacture on board and to make suggestions to overcome the troubles.

Magnetic mines were little known and there was no knowledge of the effect of an underwater explosion on electrical machinery at that time. Unfortunately, Mr. Dalton stepped on a loose plank over a grating, fell

The changes to the hull profile caused by the refit are quite visible in this picture of the ship from 1943, the most obvious being the bulges. (Imperial War Museum)

awkwardly, and had to return to Bedford before he could go aboard. It must be remembered that there was a state of blackout at the time that we visited the ship and the personnel were in a state of confusion because 650 men had been made idle and . . . alternative jobs would have to be found for them.

To an inexperienced eye, the damage did not look very great. There was a horizontal slit in the ship's side, but the wooden supports holding her upright in the dock probably made it difficult to appreciate the amount of distortion which had taken place.

W. H. Allen had supplied a large number of generators, motors, and control gear to the then current Admiralty specification, but their performance under shock conditions was unknown. It was alleged that when the main armament was being used, the relays of the starters would fall out and disconnect the circuit. . . .

It was apparent that considerable damage had been done. One hold was flooded, and carcasses of pigs and sheep were floating in the water. On the vertical motors, driving Drysdale pumps, the cast iron stools connecting the motor bases to the pump had all fractured, horizontal motors and generators had moved on their mountings, and holding down bolts had stretched. The damage to the mountings of the horizontal [machinery was] much, much less . . . as these are integral with the magnets and are of fabricated steel. . . .

All bearings were damaged due to indentation and had become noisy but could probably run for a reasonable time until they were replaced at the next refit. The roller bearings of the horizontal machines were the worst damage. . . .

As a result of the failure of electrical gear under shock conditions on this vessel, gradually a shockproof specification was introduced, and the shock requirements of each machine was specified according to its weight, height above the waterline, and the necessity for the machine to remain functional for the ship to be a fighting unit. Cast iron castings were eliminated and replaced by malleable iron or steel. Larger-diameter shafts were required, which in extreme cases were allowed to bend and hit the main poles. The machine would thus run, but probably roughly.

Because the forecastle step-down had been earlier identified as a point of weakness, additional plating was introduced there to strengthen it. The main armour belt had been removed entirely, with the additional plating installed higher up on the hull. As well as the known plans to upgrade the ship's armament and sensors, adjustments were made to ensure the ship's stability. Bulges were added running from just forward of A turret to about halfway down X turret. These provided both the stability and the additional buoyancy needed to compensate for the changes made during the repairs. This additional hull capacity would have an unanticipated result further down the line: *Belfast* would be the only British ship armed with the triple 6-inch turret to retain all four main battery emplacements. All the other ships would lose the superfiring aft X turret, either in refit or during design, to provide topweight and stability for additional radar and AA guns.

The main armour belt was then reinstalled over the bulges, which would marginally increase protection against incoming fire by absorbing splinters and blast effects should shells or bomb blasts come close to defeating the armour. A number of other minor changes were also made to the hull, primarily to improve seakeeping.

Whereas the ship had lacked radar going into her restoration, she emerged with a complete suite of equipment that included Type 281 air search radar, Type 273 surface search radar, Type 284 main and Type 285 secondary battery radar, the latter for antisurface and antiair fire control direction for the 4-inch guns; along with Type 283 "blind barrage" fire control radar for her 4-inch guns, and Type 242, 251, and 252 IFF (identification friend or foe) systems.

Additional fire control systems included rangefinders, directors, and fire control tables; remote power control (RPC) for the heavy and medium AA batteries; and the replacement of the .50-calibre light AA with 14 of the new 20-mm Oerlikons—5-in twin mountings and 4 singles. Radio direction-finding equipment and a Type 91 radar jammer designed to degrade the capabilities of enemy fire control radar added to the ship's electronic warfare arsenal.

More practical changes were also being made. Larger ready-use lockers for 4-inch ammunition reflected the rapid consumption of AA rounds by these guns in other ships as well as the ship's slightly larger overall ammunition capacity; lack of shells had been a key contributor to the loss of *Gloucester* in 1941. Additional plating was installed between the 4-inch mountings to protect the crews from splinter and blast effects that might otherwise disable multiple guns—another hard-won lesson of the war. Degaussing coils, a lesson of her own encounter with the magnetic mine, were added, along with new shock-proof machinery and mountings designed to be quickly and easily replaced should they fail.

The reconstructed *Belfast* also carried sonar (known at the time as Asdic in the Royal Navy), hoses to refuel escorting destroyers, and a ship-wide loud-hailer that allowed officers to shout at everyone aboard simultaneously.

Happily, the installation of all this new equipment coincided with the first-large scale deployment of the new centimetric radar. When *Belfast* finally emerged from Devonport, recommissioning on 3 November 1942, she incorporated almost all the wartime lessons the Royal Navy had learned thus far while also mounting some of the latest technological advancements available. This would make her a formidable foe for any enemy cruiser or destroyer, with capabilities far beyond those of the ship that had run into the mine just over two years earlier.

The interior of A turret, uniquely preserved among British cruisers, illustrates *Belfast*'s fire power. (Author's collection)

Belfast's shell hoists are still in place, with the ring of 6-inch shells ready to be fed to the turrets at any angle of rotation. (Author's collection)

BACK INTO THE FIGHT

The "new" *Belfast* sailed north from Devonport to take up her role as the flagship of the Tenth Cruiser Squadron, Home Fleet, based at Scapa Flow under Vice-Admiral Robert Burnett. Over the course of the next year she would be thrown into some of the most brutal conditions of the war, as if doing penance for missing so much of it thus far. Her missions involved a combination of Arctic convoy escort work, blockade duty, and sweeps with the Home Fleet.

Commanding from the open bridge when most of the ship was covered in ice called for heavy-duty winter clothing and plenty of hot tea! (Imperial War Museum)

George Burridge:

My first impressions of HMS Belfast *when I arrived? Well, it had been mined up in Scotland and it had been towed down to Devonport for repairs, and when we joined it, it was just completely still in the hands of dockyard mates. There were hydraulic pipes and men working all over the place. It wasn't really ready for us, but this was all part of the induction into going on a big ship like that, it was a real mess when we got there. Not at all as you would envision, just a naval ship just still being repaired.*

Belfast left Scapa to sail to Iceland, where she joined the covering force for convoy JW53. She faced the double-edged sword of incredibly rough seas and brutal temperatures. Six of the convoy ships were forced to turn back, as were two of the escorting warships: most of the roof of *Sheffield*'s A turret was peeled open like a sardine can, and the escort carrier *Dasher* had a major split in the flight deck as welds failed in the appalling cold. Fortunately, the weather also shielded the convoy from major attack. Although U-boats and the Luftwaffe made attempts at sinking the merchantmen, the heaving seas and driving winds rendered attacks almost entirely pointless. The crew enjoyed better weather returning from Russia with RA53 in early March 1943, but this also facilitated German attacks, three merchant ships being lost to U-boats on this voyage.

John Harrison:

It is so cold that you have to keep the guns, especially those antiaircraft guns, on the upper deck moving at a regular interval otherwise the grease froze up and you can't move, which is no good if you get attacked. Fortunately, we weren't attacked.

George Burridge:

The heavy, heavy seas, the first time we went seriously to sea was either January or February '43. We went out. And we were told we were going to Scapa or at least near Scapa, and we went straight out into about a Force 8 or 9 gale, and I can recall now literally seeing the whole ship strewn with bodies being seasick all over all the gangways, all the pathways, and that lasted a couple of days almost, and then either Captain Parham or Admiral Burnett himself came on the tannoy [public address system] to say not to be ashamed of what's happened because we were all sick, even the professionals; they'd never seen seas like this. It was very, very rough and nobody had anything to eat. Everybody was just lying about completely incapacitated. But the main thing about those conditions is that you're as safe as you can be because submarines can't operate in those waters, because the ship was rolling about like a cork.

Very, very cold. It was made quite clear that if you went on the upper deck . . . when it was very cold, unless you had gloves on, if you touched any part of it that was at all metal with your bare hands, then you would likely to lose the skin as your hand would just stick there. And of course there was another job, chipping ice off the off the upper deck because if it takes on too much weight, there's a distinct risk that it could capsize. So chipping ice off the guns and the upper deck, that was a fairly routine sort of job for people.

As U-boat attacks intensified in the Atlantic, more ships, both merchantmen and escorts, were diverted to that area of operations. In the aftermath of the PQ17 convoy disaster and as daylight hours in the Arctic lengthened, a much heavier escort force was deemed necessary to secure the convoys' safety. There simply weren't enough escorts to cover both Atlantic and Arctic convoys along with all the other important convoy routings, nor were the expected casualties deemed acceptable, so further convoys to the USSR were suspended until November.

Belfast spent the spring and most of the summer on blockade patrol instead. It was relatively uneventful duty in terms of enemy action but nevertheless trying for the crew. Whereas the convoy work was generally about two weeks of intense activity, the blockade patrols could last a month or more with very rapid turnarounds, often in distant austere ports such as those of Iceland. In June 1943, a combination of the foul weather, which curtailed almost all aircraft operations, and the efficacy of the ship's radar led to the removal of her Walrus aircraft. The hangar space was made available to the crew for off-duty activities—a welcomed development because the open deck spaces men looking to relax normally frequented were a combination ice-rink, roller-coaster, and death trap in the upper reaches of the Atlantic and the lower reaches of the Arctic Ocean.

Before he passed away, John Harrison, a veteran of HMS Belfast, *regularly visited the ship in the 2000s and 2010s. During these visits he was fond of recount-*

Ice buildup would not typically prevent the ship's guns from firing, but the additional weight could threaten her stability if allowed to get out of hand. (Imperial War Museum)

ing an incident when the Arctic weather simultaneously almost killed him and saved his life.

He was on his way from the forward superstructure to A turret when the ship crested a large wave and dove into the following trough, sending a wall of water surging over the bow. The breakwater was of precious little use against what seemed like half the sea coming at him, and for a moment death seemed certain—if not from the sheer force of the water's impact or being slammed against the bulkhead, then surely from the freezing temperatures in the sea, which could sap the life from a man in minutes. Most likely he'd be dead before anyone even noticed he was missing. Even if someone spotted him on his way overboard, there was precious little the ship could do to retrieve him given the weather. But as luck would have it, he was almost at the turret entrance when the wave rushed toward him, and he instinctively grabbed at the side-bar. Ordinarily this would have been of little use, since the power of the water was more than enough to rip away any man's grip, but such was the cold that his glove immediately froze solid upon contact with the metal.

Physically unable to let go even if he wanted to, poor Harrison found himself "streaming like a pennant" as the water cascaded over him. Moments later the wave passed, and after some rather motivated knocking he was admitted to the turret and handed a hot cup of tea to help kick-start his recovery.

Gordon Painter:

Well, on Russian convoy work we were issued with long johns, which were in those days about half an inch thick, and they were nice and warm. Balaclava, of course. . . . I've still got my balaclava, there's no salt on it now, but I've still got it. And of course we used to have the tot of the rum, which was very warming. Normally you had one tot a day, but in the conditions in the Arctic like it was then, that was doubled.

A layer of ice this thick could be a problem if the ship had to fire her main guns. The crew had to take care to avoid injuries when chipping it off. (Imperial War Museum)

Ice buildup could make passage along the deck tricky, but it also afforded a degree of concealment in blizzard conditions. (Imperial War Museum)

A thick coating of ice could make the scuttles and windows opaque and the ladder impassable. (Imperial War Museum)

Early July 1943 saw a welcome break from routine thanks to Operation Camera, a major deployment of Allied naval strength that simulated an invasion force heading to Norway to distract the Germans from the Allies' real invasion of Sicily. Although there was little reaction from the Germans, the operation did provide the useful intelligence that it was now possible for escorted Allied carriers to operate off Norway without significant threat of German surface forces deploying to intercept them. This information would later be used in calculating the required escort for a number of strike missions carried out against the German battleship *Tirpitz*.

These operations continued on a smaller scale. Operation FN in August was followed by Operation Lorry in early September. Lorry was a supply run to British units operating in the USSR by a pair of destroyers, for which *Belfast* and the rest of her squadron provided distant cover and a distraction by investigating Spitzbergen. In late September *Belfast* supported Operation SF, an ongoing series of sweeps aimed at intercepting U-boats that were using northern routes to get into the Atlantic, with a specific additional objective to try and hunt down a suspected blockade-runner.

Late September also saw *Tirpitz* put out of action by X-Craft (British mini-submarines), which led to the decision to launch Operation Leader, an attack on German shipping off Norway by the carrier USS *Ranger*, supported by British and American forces. While *Tirpitz* had been operating alongside *Scharnhorst*, such a deployment would have demanded escort by three or four Allied battleships to ensure a significant margin of superiority. After the withdrawal in August of the USS *South Dakota* and USS *Alabama*, the Home Fleet was left with two full-size battleships—HMS *Duke of York* and *Anson*—to protect the slower *Ranger* from *Scharnhorst*, the smaller of the two Kriegsmarine vessels, a relatively easy task.

As *Belfast* sailed as part of *Ranger*'s escort, a series of air strikes sank a number of German or German-controlled ships and disrupted shipping operations along the Norwegian coast. With this operation successfully concluded, *Belfast* spent most of the rest of October in port, conducting maintenance, allowing the crew to go on leave and cleaning out the boilers in anticipation of the Arctic convoys resuming.

George Burridge:

> *Because of being the flagship of the Tenth Cruiser Squadron, it was quite clear that we had to be that much better than the other two cruisers in the squadron. And I think discipline was tighter as a result because the officers and the petty officers were all put under extra pressure because we had the admiral, Burnett, on board. Which is understandable.*

The first of the Arctic convoys, JW/RA 54A and 54B, passed relatively uneventfully, with *Belfast* providing close cover for the first and distant cover for the second. On 15 December, along with the cruisers *Norfolk* and *Sheffield*, she provided close cover for convoy JW55A, arriving at the Kola Inlet four days later. On 22 December the trio headed back west, ostensibly covering RA55A, while JW55B headed east toward them.

But all was not quite as it seemed. The confluence of the two convoys, and more especially the sailing of JW55B with an ostensibly light escort force of only destroyers and lighter craft, was a ploy designed by Admiral Fraser to draw out the last remaining operational German capital ship, *Scharnhorst*. In fact, *Belfast* and her two companions, designated "Force 1," were to join JW55B as soon as possible, while "Force 2" with the battleship *Duke of York*, the cruiser *Jamaica*, and a number of destroyers covertly shadowed the convoy.

The Kriegsmarine took the bait. *Scharnhorst* and five destroyers sailed to intercept the convoy even as the weather closed in, rendering aerial reconnaissance impossible. This circumstance favoured the British, because they knew where their convoys were and all their larger vessels were equipped with some form of radar. The smaller German force had to try and find the convoy in the murk and had no idea about the heavy escort forces waiting for them.

SINKING *SCHARNHORST*

Somewhere in the darkness, surrounded by snow squalls, Admiral Erich Bey ordered his destroyers to detach and search for the Allied convoy. They found nothing, and indeed contributed nothing to the overall battle to come. At 0840 on 26 December 1943, *Belfast's* radar picked up *Scharnhorst* at 35,000 yards on bearing 295, less than 40 miles from the convoy. At about 0900 the radar picked up another contact, probably one of the German destroyers. But in the darkness and driving snow, anyone without a functioning radar was essentially blind, whereas in clear weather, the ships were close enough to have easily spotted each other.

George Burridge:

On the 25th we were called to action stations, and my action station was the radar plot just under the bridge. And we were simply doing our straightforward job of plotting the reports from the radar sets and then we were eventually told that we were in contact, they thought with heavy German ships or a ship and that we were likely to be going into action fairly soon. After this we had several skirmishes, they were the ships that were reported as being close enough to cause us problems. Bearing in mind the Scharnhorst *was a very powerful ship, 11-inch guns against our 6-inch guns, and it was on the 26th that I remember Admiral Burnett coming on to say that we were in contact with almost certainly the* Scharnhorst *and we were about to start firing star shell to identify the ship. And this carried on for some time, star shells were fired, our guns opened up.*

During that action, this was still early, I think, in the 26th when we had reports that the Norfolk *had been hit by the* Scharnhorst *and was temporarily put out of action, and I think they lost six men on that. It was hit after, and then we had a further report*

The embattled *Scharnhorst* fought back as best she could but was outnumbered and surrounded by ships with superior sensor systems. Once the ship had been slowed with a hit to the machinery spaces, the end was inevitable. (With permission of Joseph Reindler RN)

from the Sheffield *to say they were having engine problems and couldn't keep up with the high-speed action. I recall Admiral Burnett coming on to say that. We were at the moment alone and we were going to engage the* Scharnhorst, *which frightened the life out of everybody, I think.*

By 0915 the three cruisers had formed a line heading south as the range closed, altering course toward the east. Finally at 0921 *Sheffield* reported a visual spotting of *Scharnhorst* at 13,000 yards, almost point-blank range for ships of this period. *Belfast* and her companions opened fire and the German battleship replied in kind, but already confusion was beginning to set in.

Belfast and *Sheffield* were distinctively Town-class cruisers even in hazy profile, but they carried reduced-flash charges for their guns (often referred to as "flashless," albeit relative to the normal charge flash). *Norfolk*'s 8-inch guns were not supplied with such charges, and this meant from the Germans' perspective that the difference in the respective gun flashes was considerably larger than would be expected given the actual two-inch difference in calibre. Coupled with the fact that the County class had four twin turrets and was quite long at 632 feet, the Germans concluded that *Norfolk* was actually a *Revenge*-class battleship, a vessel that was in fact 12 feet shorter than the heavy cruiser. The main distinguishing feature, *Norfolk*'s three funnels as opposed

Weather conditions as the battle with *Scharnhorst* developed were even worse than those shown in this picture, taken during another convoy run; add darkness and snow for the full effect. (Imperial War Museum)

***Belfast* was not supposed to fight *Scharnhorst* one-on-one, but rather drive her toward the considerably more powerful *Duke of York*. (Author's collection)**

HMS *Norfolk* had taken part in the hunt for *Bismarck*, but she would not escape unscathed when she encountered *Scharnhorst*. (Author's collection)

Admiral Fraser relied on constant updates from *Belfast* to bring *Duke of York*'s big 14-inch guns into action at the right time. (Author's collection)

to a *Revenge*'s one, was concealed by the blizzard and the pale camouflage applied to the cruiser's upperworks.

Unwilling to engage what he believed to be an opponent with superior firepower and protection, Bey turned away, using his perceived best remaining asset—superior speed—to try and escape. Thanks to the misidentification, *Scharnhorst*'s speed advantage was somewhat less than Bey thought, although in the heavy weather the German battleship's greater mass meant she was still the faster ship. But before the range could open enough to cause a cessation of fire, two shells hit *Scharnhorst*. One was relatively inconsequential, but the second destroyed the forward radar array's ability to function, leaving the battleship blind in the forward arc just when the commander needed to see what was out there, having previously kept the radar off to try and sneak up on the convoy.

George Stanley:

> *We were in the turret all day long, so we had brought to us cocoa and corned beef sandwiches. Just doing the job. . . . I never thought about . . . King and country or anything like that. I was just there. Just doing a job. The day before, the admiral or the captain said that the* Scharnhorst *had put to sea, expect to make contact within the next 24 hours. Then at 0830 the following morning, action stations, and I think we opened fire about half past nine in the morning. We didn't know this at the time but there was the* Belfast, *the* Norfolk, *and the* Sheffield, *three cruisers. That's us, a 6-inch;* Sheffield, *a 6-inch, and the* Norfolk *with the 8-inch. I think it was about six or seven men killed on the* Norfolk. *The* Sheffield *had engine trouble so she fell back. So at one time the* Belfast *was the only ship in contact with the* Scharnhorst. *And I believe what saved us was we fired non-flash cordite, so I don't think the Germans knew what was out there because her radar got knocked out earlier on, and I believe if she had known that all it was, was a 6-inch cruiser chasing her, she would have turned back because she had 11-inch guns, so we would not have stood a chance.*
>
> *Then in the afternoon, that's when the* Duke of York *came up.*

With *Belfast* and the other cruisers limited to 24 knots in the mountainous seas, Admiral Burnett realised that he couldn't run down his opponent; but he was also fairly sure that the battleship would try and loop back around to attack the convoy. Thus, the three cruisers headed east to a position ten miles ahead of the convoy, probing into the darkness with their radar. Time ticked by. Local dawn arrived at 1100, and then about an hour later *Belfast* once again picked up her erstwhile opponent. At 1221 *Sheffield* established visual confirmation at 11,000 yards, and gunfire erupted once more. This time the action technically went better for *Scharnhorst*: two hits on *Norfolk* knocked out her X turret and her radar, while a near miss sent splinters into *Sheffield* that caused minor damage, although stripped gearing on her inboard port propeller shaft subsequently forced her to fall back.

The destroyers accompanying the cruisers had been sent in to attack with torpedoes, but with the German vessel withdrawing once again they were unable to get close enough to do so. Instead, they settled for a few exchanges of gunfire before falling back.

With the damage to *Sheffield* limiting her speed and the damage to *Norfolk* leaving her blind, only *Belfast* was in a position to pursue *Scharnhorst*. At 1241 both sides ceased firing. *Belfast* was able to increase speed thanks to slightly calmer sea conditions, although the driving rain and heavy snow were as bad as ever. As the range opened to 20,000 yards *Scharnhorst*'s commander appears to have taken the lack of firing from the British to signify loss of contact. Meanwhile, on board *Belfast* it had been noted that the German ship's new course was leading her toward Force 2. In order not to spook Bey into changing course, *Belfast* simply followed while sending a steady stream of position reports to Admiral Fraser. Of course, the fact that *Belfast* stood very little chance if she were to go one-on-one with a battleship probably also had something to do with the lack of further gunfire.

By 1600 *Belfast* was completely alone, *Sheffield* and *Norfolk* both having fallen back. But the net was closing. At 1617, thanks in large part to *Belfast*'s constant reports, *Duke of York*'s radar picked up the incoming *Scharnhorst*. Fraser's destroyers now moved to engage with torpedoes while *Sheffield* gradually began to close the distance that had opened between her and *Belfast*. The range continued to tick down until at 1637 Fraser ordered *Belfast* to open fire with star shell to illuminate the target and provide a distraction while *Duke of York* continued her stealthy approach.

Belfast began firing at 1647, the illumination rounds showing an enemy with guns trained fore and aft, caught completely unaware. *Duke of York*'s 5.25-inch also fired star shell a minute later, and within a couple of minutes the British battleship's 14-inch guns let loose with the first of many salvos starting at 12,000 yards. The first salvo scored a direct hit, knocking out *Scharnhorst*'s "Anton" turret while splinters and water rained down from near misses.

Gordon Painter:

It was Christmas and I remember firing, the Belfast *fired flares to light up the ocean, of course, to spot the* Scharnhorst. *We actually picked her up on the radar, on the radar screen. We then fired broadside at her, I'm not sure the number since that's too long ago. I believe we fired three torpedoes at her; one of the destroyers finished her off eventually. I do remember the* Scharnhorst *firing back and I remember some of the shells falling around us, not too far from us.*

I think most when you're in action like that your mind goes back to back home, and I do remember saying to myself, "Well, this is Christmas, and back home if they've got the food coupons to get their food, they're having a Christmas dinner and party." But we weren't having a party, far from it. . . .

After the Scharnhorst *was sunk, we did pick up, I think it was 36 survivors. I have a copy of their signatures. They were in fairly good shape, naturally suffering from the cold and that sort of thing. I don't know very much about them, but they were transferred then from us to another ship. It wouldn't have been a hospital ship, not up there, a destroyer or something would have taken them and got them back quicker.*

George Burridge:

I was in the plot recording the positions of all our ships and the enemy ships as well. That was my job, and that continued until the actual battle with the Scharnhorst started. The Duke of York was coming out from Scapa or from the south. We knew that they were coming out to reinforce us, otherwise we would have not lasted long at all, quite frankly. And our guns were firing on and off for quite a long time. We were going in firing and coming out again to hopefully keep out of range, and at one stage, about halfway through, I recall this quite clearly, the armoured door, which was a sliding armour door to the plot, was blown off. We thought we'd been hit, but it was our own guns that were firing, the A and B turrets were firing aft and the shock had blown the door off. So we were exposed to everything. It was just blown off, and for the rest of the battle, we were literally able to see what was going on firsthand because the plot door was open and obviously we can't stop and go about putting that back on. Firing continued and then of course the Duke of York started firing, and I can see it now. The entire Scharnhorst on fire from bow to stern, literally just a mass of flames, and we in due course ended with torpedo attacks. Went in with torpedo attacks two or three times and then there were so many other ships

***Scharnhorst* survivors disembarking from a British ship after the battle. (Imperial War Museum)**

there, destroyers and cruisers, that we pulled away and the destroyers went in to finish it off. We didn't expect to pick up any survivors, but we did see little red lights in the water, but we were pulling away so that the destroyers could finish the ship off, and they did pick up about 36 survivors from the Scharnhorst, that's all.

With *Duke of York* and *Jamaica* firing from the south, *Belfast* opened fire from the north, soon joined by *Norfolk*, which had been making best speed to catch up. *Belfast* prepared to launch a torpedo attack, but after it was clear he was boxed in to the north and south, Bey ran east, opening the range again as the cruisers, *Duke of York*, and various destroyers all tried to chase him down. Despite their best efforts *Scharnhorst* drew slowly out of range of *Belfast*'s 6-inch guns. Ceasefire sounded on *Belfast* at 1742, but just after 1800 a shell from *Duke of York* arced down through *Scharnhorst*'s armour and disabled one of the boiler rooms. The German battleship immediately lost speed and rapidly came back into range of first *Belfast*'s main guns, then her torpedoes, which she fired at 1927, along with numerous torpedoes from the pack of destroyers that were likewise now able to close in.

At some point between 1940 and 1945, hit by numerous shells and torpedoes, *Scharnhorst* rolled over and sank, leaving the heavy cruiser *Lutzow* as the single largest threat to the Allied convoys, at least until *Tirpitz* could be repaired. For the moment, this massively reduced the amount of forces the Allies needed to commit to the Arctic theatre.

Having used a lot of fuel in the pursuit, the cruisers headed back to the Kola Inlet to top up their tanks. *Belfast* also collected 19 tons of Russian silver before heading back to Scapa in company with *Sheffield* and *Norfolk*. With no need to escort convoys against heavy German surface units, the three ships made the run at high speed. They reached Scapa on the first day of 1944 and took on ammunition and stores before heading down to Rosyth for some well-earned shore leave.

Arthur Fursland:

They made a statement over the tannoy system: "The Scharnhorst should have put at sea." So from then onward the galley was closed down, that was everything clamped down. So that day went by, Christmas Day went by largely quietly because the crew knew what was on.

Then came Boxing Day, quarter to nine in the morning, that's 0845 navy time. Action stations bugle. The padre give us short service of prayer and we all had to go to our action stations. Well, my place was down the port diesel. So I went down there and that's where I stayed for 12 hours. It wasn't a short while before she fired a whole broadside, engaged there with radar. The first to go was the chief. They come down and start up the pumps and left me, I was clamped up each side by watertight doors and just a hatch to get down.

And the first broadside to the Belfast fired . . . the vibration of the ship . . . and again. Now the two central pumps were out of action, fuses gone, I've seen the temperatures rising up. I thought, oh good grief. Luckily . . . between the two bulkhead doors was a firehose and a fire main with the hose hung on a rung, so I undid that, pulled it over the hatches, down the hatch, down to the deck level, and up on the bypass. I didn't know how I did it, I just had to do it. I circulated water from the saltwater pump mains through the engine for 8 to 12 hours.

The only thing I worried about was being on my own. No disrespect to the people on the bridge of ships, guns, crews, and all like that. They had their mates around them get killed, no doubt. But me and my mate on the other side as well were on our own.

Eventually we got into Murmansk. We stayed here for a few days and the Russians give us a reindeer. They had the aircraft hangar. . . . Then the crew started exercising, trying out the guns again, you know; the reindeer went mad. So the butchers had to kill them, so we had reindeer for Christmas.

The Battle of the North Cape was the only time *Belfast* got to exercise her torpedo launchers against their intended targets. (Imperial War Museum)

Belfast expended a considerable amount of ammunition in the fight with *Scharnhorst*, which would have been tallied on these boards in the respective turrets' shell rooms and magazines. (Author's collection)

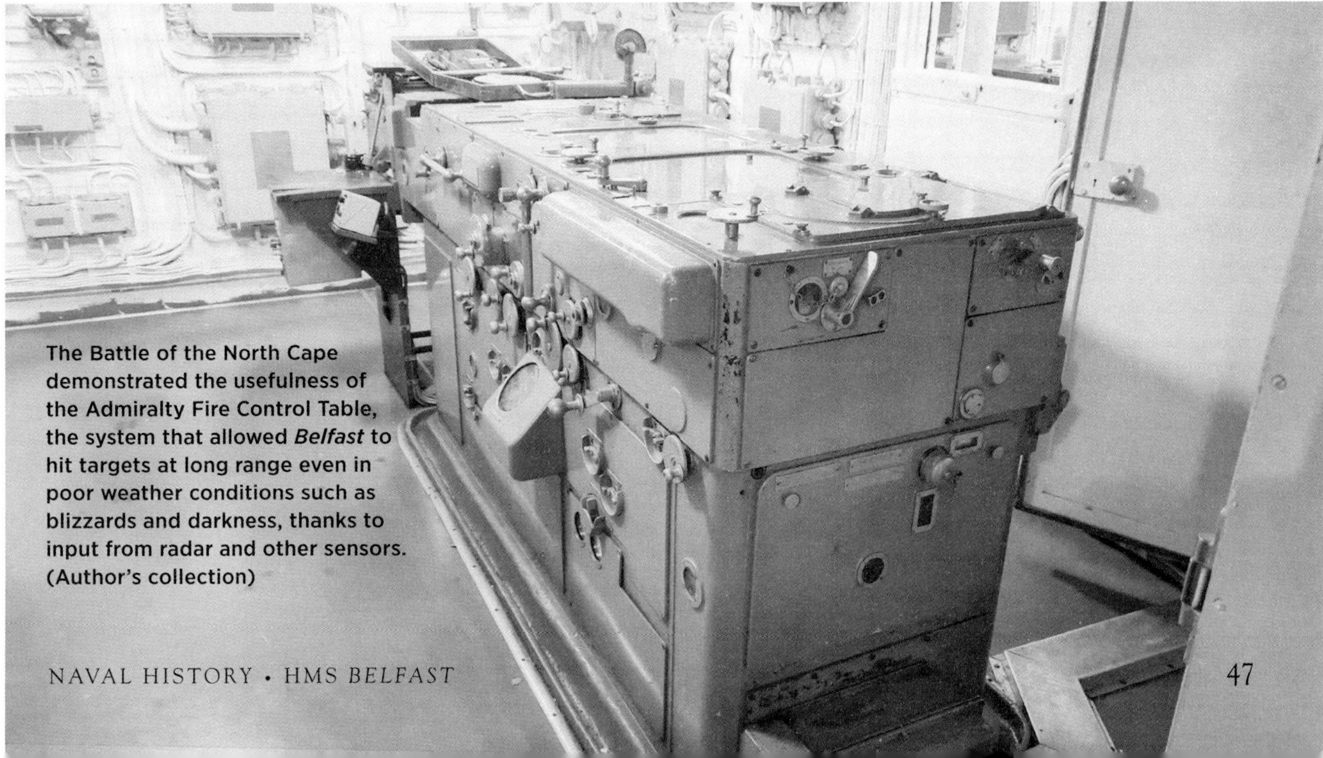

The Battle of the North Cape demonstrated the usefulness of the Admiralty Fire Control Table, the system that allowed *Belfast* to hit targets at long range even in poor weather conditions such as blizzards and darkness, thanks to input from radar and other sensors. (Author's collection)

TAGGING *TIRPITZ*

As the crew filtered back aboard the ship, news came through that *Tirpitz* had been repaired and was now in Altenfjord. This could be a significant problem both for the renewed Arctic convoys and for upcoming operations planned to liberate France. With an operational *Tirpitz* on the loose, significant naval forces would have to be committed to keep the convoys safe just at the time when ships in large numbers were needed in the Channel.

But thanks to operations the previous year, a path was now open to the Allies to close off the threat once more, at least temporarily. This took the form of Operation Tungsten. Once again Admiral Fraser split his ships into two strike forces. After ensuring convoy JW58 made it through safely they headed for their primary target. The battleship *Anson* along with *Belfast*, *Jamaica*, and six destroyers escorted the fleet carriers *Furious* and *Victorious*, each loaded with Barracuda strike aircraft; while HMS *Royalist* led the escort carriers *Emperor*, *Searcher*, *Pursuer*, and *Fencer*, fully loaded with American-made F6F Hellcats and F4U Corsairs to provide the fighter screen.

The massed air strike began on 3 April 1944, with low-flying fighter sweeps supressing the German AA guns while the Barracudas came in behind, dropping a mix of 1,600-pound AP bombs aimed at the ship and 500-pound delayed-action bombs aimed to explode alongside. Although not sunk, *Tirpitz* was once again put out of action, and resources could now be focused farther south—all at the cost of a single lost Barracuda. A follow-up strike on 25 April to try to sink *Tirpitz* had to be called off due to bad weather over the target, and the strike force had to be contented with picking off some German cargo ships instead.

With *Tirpitz* out of action again, there was time for a brief refit. By this stage in the war *Belfast* had lost the twin 20-mm Oerlikon mount atop B turret, exchanged for a number of additional single 20-mms that had gradually been brought aboard over the past year or so.

(above) *Belfast* is just visible to the starboard aft quarter of HMS *Victorious*, which is recovering her aircraft after attacking *Tirpitz*. (Imperial War Museum)

D-DAY

In the run-up to D-Day, *Belfast* was being prepared to take part in the shore bombardment supporting the landings on Gold and Juno beaches. While the invasion of Normandy is widely known as Operation Overlord, that name refers to the amphibious landings themselves; the naval element was known as Operation Neptune. Unknown to the crew as they prepared for the battle, the ship was the subject of a political storm back in London.

Prime Minister Winston Churchill had declared that he wished to be present for the invasion on D-Day. General Dwight Eisenhower, who was in overall control of the operation, responded with an absolute refusal. The landings would be extremely difficult and casualties were likely to be high, and he could not spare the forces to babysit a politician in a landing craft. Churchill was not used to not getting his way. He informed Eisenhower that while the American officer might control the army, he had no control over the administration of the Royal Navy. If one Winston Spencer Churchill, His Majesty's subject, wished to join a ship's company, there was nothing the U.S. Army or even the U.S. president could do to stop him.

Churchill chose *Belfast* as his vehicle, both because she would be the Force E flagship and also because she would be positioned about as close as a warship was going to get to the landings themselves, with the exception of some destroyers. He announced his decision to the First Lord of the Admiralty and the First Sea Lord, Andrew Cunningham, and made it clear to both men that he would brook no further opposition. Cunningham, a hardened Royal Navy veteran, refused to be intimidated. Churchill was in his view less intimidating than the Regia Marina's battleships, and Cunningham hadn't backed down from them either. When Churchill waved aside Cunningham's objections, King George VI himself stepped in to resolve the situation. If Churchill was going to attend as prime minister of the United Kingdom, the King said, then it was only proper that he should attend as well in his role as commander in chief of the British armed forces. While apparently heedless of his own safety, Churchill could not place the King in danger of being injured or killed by German return fire on his watch. But since the King was also Churchill's boss, he could not be ordered, only advised. Churchill for once did not get his way. The King would stay only if Churchill stayed; if he went, so would the King. In the end both men stayed behind. Meanwhile, *Belfast*'s crew prepared for their bombardment duties completely unaware of the major headache they had just avoided.

Of course, the King had actually gotten one-up on Churchill, having just returned from a Fleet Review where he'd toured the fleet from *Belfast*, which thus flew the Royal Standard for the duration of the ceremony.

Belfast left the Clyde on 2 June in company with *Warspite*, *Ramillies*, *Roberts*, 4 cruisers, and 15 destroyers with the objective of being offshore at 0530 on the fifth,

(above) *Belfast* opens fire with her 4-inch guns off the coast of Normandy in support of the Allied landings. (Imperial War Museum)

when the landings were scheduled to take place. The weather off Normandy proved to be awful that night, and the landings were postponed until the following day, leaving *Belfast* and the other ships sailing up and down the Irish Sea until the weather south of them improved. They arrived at the Solent between the UK mainland and the Isle of Wight in good time for the revised schedule before heading south through mine-swept channels to take up station.

Gordon Painter:

> *We came down the Irish Sea, then making down the Channel. And as you know D-Day was put off 24 hours or 48 hours [24 hours is correct], and I remember we had to hang around in the very choppy sea for this length of time. But then following night and day and night, we came down to the Channel and hence we went over during the night to start the D-Day landings.*
>
> *We were, if you like, the spearhead, . . . very honoured I suppose, in a way. We were the first ship to start the bombardment [on time, that is; a few other ships had opened fire ahead of schedule]. Although the Royal Air Force had done a marvellous job, I do remember, before we were locked in the turrets, I do remember the sky being lit up over France with the fire started by the Air Force bombing. I also remember seeing hundreds and hundreds of landing craft and small ships going across. . . . And then as I say, we started our bombardment. About 5:30 that morning, which went on for I think it must have been a good week, maybe more.*
>
> *We had a spotter plane which was attached to us. Who that guy was I'll never know, of course. But it would have been nice to have met him. He would radio back to the Belfast to tell us exactly where our salvos were dropping, whether we were short of the targets or beyond. I remember being told once that we were attacking . . . a series of tank squadrons. Anyway, these tanks were approaching the British Army, of course, who were our soldiers who had landed. I remember attacking them and being told we were scoring some good direct hits. This came from the aircraft.*
>
> *And then there was in another case, there was a church we were bombarding south of Caen . . . that the Germans were using to store ammunition. That was a target that we had to hit, which we did. Sort of proud of it, I think, when one has to fight for their country. You just have to do a job and you have to do as you're told. And these guys we're shooting at are human beings, the same as we were. When you were that age it didn't really sink home to you exactly what it was all about, and we were sad in doing some of the things we had to do. But we were doing it for the freedom and everything that this country deserves, and the future of this country.*
>
> *The bombardment was quite noisy. Of course we were firing broadsides, which means that all the guns were fired together, the whole lot. It sort of rocks the ship backward a bit, and this is continually going on, I think we did have earplugs or something in your ears because if you didn't, you'd suddenly go deaf. It was some experience.*
>
> *You can hear other ships shooting, all sorts of things going on around you. When we first got there, there were German aircraft flying at us, not very successfully, although some of the smaller ships got hit. But they soon quieted them down. I think the Royal Air Force got them. That made the job much more, I don't want to say simple because nothing was simple. But it*

***Belfast* in June 1944 heading for the Normandy beaches. Many ships expended their magazines and had to sail back to England to reload, often repeatedly, in addition to taking casualties ferried from the beaches home for further treatment. (Imperial War Museum)**

made the job easier than it would have been, let's put it that way.

The only time you could leave the turret is if nature called. And then you had somebody to take over for you. So I didn't directly see a lot that was going on.

Denis Watkinson:

We first entered the Channel just before evening time and we could see the all the convoys of ships with barrage balloons over the top of them all coming out the ports and that. We started to sail amongst them. We had to cut through all these fleets, there was 33 cruisers all together. That night it got dark and we could just see the faint outlines of all these ships and also looking at the French coast, the bombers were bombing and you could see the planes. Some had been brought down and eventually, as light was breaking, we were on our own. Our convoys were well behind us, the landing craft and the like, and we've spread out, the cruisers were spread out along the beaches.

It looked ever so peaceful after seeing all the fires and the bombing during the night. We were going to . . . head for a marker buoy. This must have been planned long before we got there, the distance toward the tower target was the batteries that were sure to try and hit us. So they put them out of action so that the troops coming to land would have a better chance of getting ashore with less casualties.

The Germans thought we wouldn't invade because it would have to be done with the tide in because that meant less chance of getting killed before you got to the beach. But they did the opposite, they did it with the tide out, which meant that we couldn't get any further in to shore.

Full action stations would be about five o'clock or something like. I mean, we were more or less at action stations all night. There isn't much expectancy because you're so busy doing what you've got to do. And you seem to block any feelings out while you're doing this. You're not sitting thinking, "Oh, I hope I don't get it. Hope this don't do it. Hope you don't do that." You get on with it, it doesn't feel like anything. It just feels that you've got to do this and you hope you're doing it right. And you never think, "Oh, well, we might get the next one" or things like that. I don't know why, there's something in the nature of people which blocks out that sort of thing.

It depends on your situation, though; you're in a big ship and you're behind the big guns, which changes your thinking altogether. When we opened fire, the first thing we had open up was X and Y turrets. We'll be opening up in five minutes (on the 4-inch guns) and then they opened fire. Well, that's when things got started and because the Germans were taken by surprise; it took a bit but then they started to fire back.

But they were mainly concerned with when the landing parties came and the merchant ships, things like that, they were the main targets; for all they had to go at us and all the warships, they were more concerned with stopping the men getting to shore.

Each ship had a spotter. He goes ashore to do that, and he telegraphs back to the ship . . . to fire so many salvos here and so many there, there's things he wants to put out of action and things like that, but we lost ours. We did get another one back, you know, sufficient to keep us going, but we knew what happened to the first one. We didn't even know his name because he was just there for that special job.

I forget the name of the battery we were firing at, but we put that out of action and then we've got the lads coming. You could see the ships coming in the distance, you know, the barrage balloons over the top of all the ships and eventually the big ships came and the landing craft was getting off the big ships lining up, and then they went in.

And we got, you could see a lot of people not getting ashore and boats getting hit and things like this blowing up and flames in the water and things like that. After we got in a position where we couldn't fire any more on the beaches, we were waiting for targets from artillery spotters and that beyond them. So we were having to fire over the top of the men. Then you're working with the army all the time, and they were giving you what targets they wanted. They just say we're being held up at such and such a place, request so many salvos, you know, and then they would say target destroyed and move further on.

I always remember seeing the Americans later, there's a landing craft full of black people, mostly black people, and they went past us. Well, we've been there from the very beginning, they were coming in while it was all clear. The Army-Navy cooperation was first class.

I've talked to quite a lot of lads who were in our line of fire and things like that, and they said it was marvellous when you heard these shells going over, said it's like a tram is going over the top of you. They said they did the job that they were wanting doing, high rate of fire with a good accuracy.

No enemy aircraft at first, but you did get a few come round later, but Spitfires helped to clear some of them out.

You could just see on the beach, you couldn't see further past it, obviously because of the buildings and other places, and the beaches weren't all that massive, especially when the tide was in. We settled down well the first night with the fleet's smokescreen around us to try and hide us because we're getting bombed. Night was our worst time if you were on 4-inch guns. Because we were found nearly every night when you could see. We did manage to get some, especially when I was on lookout, we hit one and he was on fire, and he was circling round and round and getting low and loud and I thought, "God, hope he gets done before he gets to us." Then he hits the sea and there's bodies in the water next morning, you can tell they're men because they have the leather jackets on.

Well, in the morning, the minesweepers are supposed to have gone round; during the night, apart from bombing, they used to drop mines amongst us, and the Swift came in and she was only about 100 yards away from us when she came off the beach and she sat right on a mine. You'd think somebody just cut her in two like that. She went down at once with both ends sticking up. We put nets out for anybody who wanted to scramble aboard. After that we were constantly firing and thought obviously we ought to get our midnight rations, and with no food, we're eating chocolate bars out of the canteen with nothing left.

But anyway, it seemed funny when we got back there's one of the crew's homes near the ship, and the skipper let him go ashore as long as you come back within so many hours, once they got the ship all filled up again. And when he got in, his mother says, "God, what are you doing here, I've just been listening to the wireless. Lord Haw Haw said he sunk you." Well, Lord Haw Haw was right in a way, because when we moved out, another light cruiser [it was actually a destroyer] moved in. And I think it was manned by a Polish crew, mostly Polish; then they got it. It sank but it was still showing above water.

They put a smokescreen down, but it was terrible because it was all getting inside the ship. It does make you cough if you get in an enclosed place, you're not so bad if it spreads around.

But anyway we survived the first night because it was pretty heavy and we'd have to come back to that beat because we've had to go down to the American beaches and fired so many salvoes there and then made our way back to it. When we were firing (off the American beaches) it was all cliffs and you couldn't see anything and the beach was only small. And they were getting slaughtered, so they must have asked for our assistance, from their admiral to the other admiral [who] was in charge of our three. And then we had to come back to ours, to work with the army. It was pretty much terrible for the Americans. To this day I can't understand what man with any sense would allow them to try and get off that beach and get up there when they could just throw bombs down or broadsides, what we were doing. It was terrible.

They brought some ships in, old warships, all at once and sank them to make it like a little harbour off the beach; They come under their own steam, then they just sank them and they lay on the bottom because they used the tops as a place where you could get off and then get a boat and then go the Mulberry harbour.

Then I was picked, with me being on S2 (second starboard-side twin 4-inch), and Peter, a stoker, maybe a cook, and someone else. Oh, must have been about

50 of us altogether, and they say, "You're going to shore on Juno Beach." To try and help them because the beach is getting littered. We were only supposed to be there a couple of days but stayed . . . for six weeks. It was a frontline beach, so it wouldn't move.

So, these launches came out for us, you could see where there was shelling, so the officer in charge says, "Look, we're not going to make it." So we went back to the ship. Next morning, the landing party got in these launches again first thing in the morning, we got food with us, took our own food. We got to this breakwater that was made with these sunken ships. We went around to where there's more boats from other ships all trying to help out. One got hit just further up from us. I lay down on the bottom of that boat and I prayed.

Then the army then came with some of the DUKWs and says, "Right, jump in here and we're getting ashore." And we've got on these things and the lad driving said, "Well, lie down on the bottom as much as you can. We'll get you ashore, don't worry." So he did, he got us ashore. But there was constant shelling all the time and that was like that for six weeks on that beach.

We eventually got off the beach. We had to go along this lane and turned into a big field where they were dumping all the German stuff. I remember seeing German tanks and there were little beetle tanks they used to radio control and blow them up when they got in anywhere near us, you know they're a marvellous thing, it's just like a proper tank, tracks on and everything.

The various task forces were due to commence their barrage at 0530 on 6 June, but a number of ships opened up earlier than that. *Belfast* is often mentioned among the half-dozen or so contenders for "first ship to open fire on D-Day," but her log reveals that while she did start firing three minutes early, her crew had observed at least one other ship open up four minutes before them.

Her first targets were a battery of German howitzer emplacements covering the beaches. But with preplanned coordinates and at a relatively short range (for a warship) of six miles, the ship's guns made deliberate work of suppressing the enemy emplacements. The troops who subsequently landed some hours later found the battery mostly disabled and the crews still largely hiding in their bunkers.

Belfast was able to use both her 6-inch and 4-inch guns because the range was close enough, and for most land-based targets even the smaller guns were quite substantial, the approximate continental equivalents being 100 or 105-mm. Usually classed as medium artillery, the 6-inch was equated with a 150-mm weapon that generally was referred to as heavy artillery. *Belfast* had plenty of both.

Artist impression of *Belfast* supporting the landings later in the morning of 6 June 1944. In real life, landing craft, fast-attack craft, and cruisers tended to keep a slightly wider spacing, but there were a few close calls. (Imperial War Museum)

***Belfast* opens fire on D-Day in this still photo captured from film footage shot early on the morning on 6 June 1944. (Imperial War Museum)**

But her role was not just to serve as a floating artillery emplacement. *Belfast* was also one of the nearest vessels to the beach with a fully equipped sick bay and medical staff, and by lunchtime on 6 June casualties were already being ferried back from the beach. As the landings turned into advances farther inland, *Belfast* shifted her support to a mixture of pre-mapped and on-the-spot objectives, the latter called in from ashore by troops in need of aid. During this initial period Force E was relatively little troubled by enemy activity apart from a brief torpedo attack by E-boats that was seen off by HMS *Warspite*. *Belfast* often found herself paired up with another ship patrolling the shore looking for targets, the *Dido*-class HMS *Diadem* being a frequent companion in the opening week. But as the assault entered its second week *Belfast* began running out of ammunition and was forced to return to Portsmouth to restock her magazines. She would end up doing this run again later in the operation.

Returning on 18 June, *Belfast* joined up with various cruisers, monitors, and battleships. The areas most in need of support had now moved far enough inland that only the guns of cruisers and larger ships were capable of accurate fire at the required ranges. By this stage the Germans' response to the naval forces had strengthened somewhat, and mines and small submerged attack craft became an additional hazard. During the day the fleet's lookouts could spot most threats, but at night even radar was of limited use. Many of the craft remaining to the Kriegsmarine were so small that they were difficult to spot before it was too late. Thus, the various bombardment groups formed up under a smokescreen most nights to conceal their positions.

As June ended with no major disasters, the situation felt a little safer. Some of the crew went ashore to help clear the beaches. On a night in early July *Belfast* was riding at anchor under the moonlight, clear of the sheltering smoke. Somewhat uneasy about this situation, Captain Frederick Parham asked Rear-Admiral Dalrymple-Hamilton, late of HMS *Rodney* and her fight with *Bismarck*, for permission to move back

***Belfast* was in good company off Normandy. Here the veteran battleship HMS *Warspite* adds her guns to the bombardment. (Imperial War Museum)**

into cover. The admiral, who seemed to treat almost every ship under his command as a destroyer of a slightly different size, agreed, and the ship relocated. Just as she was settling into the new position, enemy signals from Le Havre to a unit of E-boats were intercepted directing them to *Belfast*'s old position and mentioning her by name. It was a lucky escape.

Gordon Painter:

We were there after the troops were, I think it was six miles inland. . . . As we were anchored some 5 or 6 miles offshore and her range was about 14 miles, after our troops were inland about 6 miles we were no more use as we couldn't carry on bombarding. We became our own chaps and so they sent us ashore to do a bit of clearing up on the beaches. Wasn't a lot; the main part of the clearing up had been done, casualty-wise. I think the medical people had done that before we got there.

But there's all sorts of other things. Part of ships that have been broken up, guys' equipment that they've lost. I assumed a lot of the soldiers had been killed and lost their gear and there's all that sort of thing to clear up.

We had time to walk up onto the land and along to the seafront. Off the beach the houses had all been bombed, of course. I think the bombers did more of that damage than we did because we were bombarding farther inland than that. But we went into some of the houses that had been absolutely shattered, blown to bits. I picked up one or two souvenirs. I remember on one occasion there was a couple of pictures of Shirley Temple, so no doubt it must have been in a child's bedroom or something. Picked up a couple of German letters which I assume had been written to their French girlfriends. I don't read or speak German, so I'm afraid I can't translate them.

That was only a couple of days, I believe, because there isn't a lot to do after that. I mean, we were on Juno Beach, where the Canadians, I think, were landed.

The Allied lines had by now advanced so far inland that even *Belfast* was out of range and had to move east to keep up with the troops advancing in that direction. Along with *Rodney* and *Roberts* she supported Operation Charnwood, part of the attack on Caen, on 8 July. But with many lines of advance now completely out of range of ship-based gunnery and much of the Allied armies' own artillery ashore, her job was finished. She fired her guns for the last time in anger in World War II and headed north for a major refit.

Belfast had been earmarked to head east to join the war against Japan and would need all the newest gear Allied scientists had to offer. Although she had barely been at sea a year and a half after emerging from her rebuilding, newer and better radar, AA guns, and other systems were already available.

This refit was the first time a major sacrifice had to be made in the ship's larger-calibre weapons. Although her greater size and displacement meant she was able to keep all four of her 6-inch turrets, the aftmost twin 4-inchers were removed, not because the air threat was any less—indeed, the Japanese kamikazes posed some of the most lethal aerial threats of the war—but simply to save weight given the upgrades that were being made elsewhere.

***Belfast* shortly after concluding operations off Normandy in the camouflage paint pattern she wore at this stage of World War II. (Imperial War Museum)**

PREPARING FOR THE PACIFIC

Although the Kriegsmarine's surface fleet was a largely spent force, the need for ships in the Far East was growing and the Imperial Japanese Navy remained something of a threat.

Gordon Painter:

When we came back to England, we went up into Scapa Flow again. We weren't told where we were going to go, but we were issued with tropical kit and so one only had to put two and two together and realise that we were off somewhere else like the Far East. They fitted us out with air conditioning and maybe took out some of the heated pipes, which if you're going Far East naturally you will not need, but they wouldn't let us go home at all, we couldn't have any leave at all. Then we went out to sea for trials again because they took off some of the 4-inch guns [and] they fitted us out with something else and so we went to sea for trials on these. I seem to remember we were out working with submarines for a while.

Denis Parkinson:

We knew were going to the Far East because of what they did, we had 12 4-inch in 6 mounts, each a twin 4-inch. So they took 2, S3, and P3 off the aft end and they put a lot more small arms on both sides of us; we had quite a lot of pom-poms and . . . things like that because of the Japanese suicide bombers. And that was all done for that purpose; we knew they had guns fitted anywhere they could fit a gun.

But you never tend to sit and ponder about anything like that. You just said to your mate, "Hey, you fancy that? See what they're doing now!" and that would be the end of it.

Upgrades began with the four remaining twin 4-inch installations, which were modified to incorporate Remote Power Control (RPC) to allow a better integration with the new upgraded AA fire control systems being installed (and the existing systems being upgraded). On either side of the mainmast were the octuple 40-mm pom-poms, again with RPC control. Two additional quadruple pom-poms, also with RPC, supplemented the two already installed, along with four single pom-poms.

Twin and single 20-mm Oerlikons were also variously installed and re-sited around the ship; the lack of 40-mm Bofors guns was probably due to availability issues. But as it turned out, the pom-pom, sometimes derided as a short-range also-ran compared with the 40-mm Bofors, offered significant advantages against kamikazes. Chief among them was that the guns' belt-fed ammunition gave them up to a minute of continuous firing time, which, combined with the sheer volume of shells the pom-poms could throw out (especially the octuple mounting), could essentially disassemble an incoming aircraft in mid-flight, especially if it was coming straight at them. While the 40-mm Bofors was also effective against these suicide attacks, it was designed for a more conventional environment in which major damage would force a pilot to evade or break off. In the insane air environment of the 1944–45 Pacific, there was no such thing as overkill when it came to antiaircraft firepower.

Another thing to go was the aircraft-handling facilities. Although the aircraft themselves hadn't been used for some time, the catapults, the pair of heavy-duty cranes, and the hangar space were still there. All but one crane were removed; the survivor was relocated to help with handling the ship's boats, which themselves were partially relocated into the former aircraft launching area. The hangar was converted into accommodations for the additional crew the upgrades were bringing aboard, although it is still possible to trace elements of the old aircraft facilities on the ship today by following lines of patched plating and the like, which reflect the speed at which the refit was accomplished.

(left) The octuple pom-pom proved remarkably effective against kamikazes. (Imperial War Museum)

(below) With a new paint scheme and upgraded radar, *Belfast* prepares to head to the Pacific in mid-1945 after her latest refit, prepared for the anticipated swarms of conventional and kamikaze aircraft the Japanese would be throwing at the Allied fleets. (Imperial War Museum)

Better late than never, *Belfast* cruises in the deep waters of the Pacific shortly after the end of World War II. (Imperial War Museum)

This further slimming procedure allowed for a full array of radar to be fitted, with long-range search covered by Type 281B and Type 277 sets and closer-range searching done by a Type 293 array; a pair of Type 274 arrays provided gunnery control data for the 6-inch guns. Six sets of Type 282, four sets of Type 283, and three sets of Type 285 provided a full range of AA control data for the ship as a whole, and in most cases for individual gun mountings. IFF systems were also fitted. The sophisticated electronic search equipment made many of the large searchlights largely unnecessary, and most were removed as well.

Belfast emerged from her refit a couple of weeks before the war ended in Europe. After some initial exercises to familiarize the crew with the new systems, she headed for the Far East in June 1945. In early August she arrived in Australia, where some of her 20-mm Oerlikons were swapped for 40-mm Bofors guns. But even as this work was being carried out, the bombing of Hiroshima and Nagasaki led to the Japanese government's announcement of its willingness to surrender. Japan formally surrendered in mid-August.

Gordon Painter:

We were heading out [to the] Far East; we saw England for the last time for we didn't know how long. We didn't quite really know what the future was going to hold. So we then went to Gibraltar, where we picked up more stores, and then we went on through to Malta. There they fitted us up with more of the U.S. Bofors. How many? I don't know, but they were on top of some of the turrets.

We were in Malta for nearly a month, and then from there we went to Port Said through the Suez Canal to Port Suez, Aden, Colombo, and then straight through to Fremantle in Australia. This was when the Japanese surrendered, just as we got to that end.

We were very relieved because I think we were a bit more concerned about going into the Japanese war than we were back home in Europe. But on arriving at Fremantle you might've thought it was us that had won the war right there because we were greeted with open arms and we were all given a weekend's leave, 48 hours' leave, and as we stepped off the gangplank where the ship was we would grab local people and say, "What are you doing on the weekends?"

"Well, nothing."

"Are you coming with us, then?"

And we had a whale of a time. I think the parties all started that evening and went on to Sunday night, and we met back on board on Monday morning. But they were very good to us so. I had my own bedroom in this place ashore.

Weekend passes and parties aside, the ship wasn't able to stand down completely. The battleship USS *Pennsylvania* had been hit and almost sunk by a Japanese torpedo bomber in the gap between the announcement of Japan's intent to surrender and the actual surrender itself, and all Allied vessels conducted themselves as if the war was still going in full force. No doubt Admiral William "Bull" Halsey's words to the U.S. Third Fleet resonated in the British Pacific Fleet (BPF): "Cessation of hostilities. War is over. . . . If any Japanese airplanes appear, shoot them down in a friendly way."

Belfast was not present for the official surrender of Japan as a number of the other BPF units were. She had been directed to the Chinese coast to assist in the release, care, and transport of Allied prisoners of war. Most of them were malnourished and in extremely poor health, having been placed in work camps and prisons in territory occupied by the Japanese along the eastern coast of Asia.

Gordon Painter:

When we left Fremantle we returned to Sydney. We had ten days, I think, in Sydney and then to the north to Formosa [Taiwan]. The Japanese hadn't surrendered in Formosa, they wouldn't accept defeat and they kept on fighting. I remember we had to do a bit of guard duty on the gangway as we tied up alongside the jetty and I remember being shot at there by a couple of Japanese snipers.

They must have missed, otherwise I wouldn't be here, would I? What we went there for mainly was to take off the British prisoners that the Japanese were holding. I don't remember the numbers or anything. But I always remember somebody saying that they looked in worse condition than the prisoners did in Britain. Knowing the Japanese of the day, I quite believe it.

This work occupied the ship for the rest of the year. *Belfast* would not truly feel the effects of the war's end until the start of 1946.

Belfast in Portsmouth in 1948. (Author's collection)

A BRIEF PERIOD OF PEACE

The environment the British sailors encountered in the Far East was an abrupt change for men accustomed to serving in the North Atlantic. They had to learn to deal with heat, humidity, typhoons, and boredom.

Gordon Painter:

It was terribly hot—very, very hot. It was there that we saw some of the roughest seas that we [had] ever seen. And we honestly all thought that the Belfast was going to go down with it, but she's a grand old ship and she rode it out. The seas were very, very high, very heavy. Some of the waves were going over the top of the bridge, which is quite a height.

But as I say, as a younger person you don't have the same sense of danger, it's more excitement really than danger. But there comes a time when you can't run anywhere you want on board a ship. There's no place to go to get away from the heat; it was sticky, it was hot, humid. But with the air conditioning that we had in the mess, it wasn't quite like the Savoy Hotel in London but it was liveable.

My harbour job, as we call it, was as a sailmaker's mate for my sins. I quite enjoyed being a sailmaker's mate, repairing awnings mainly, and naturally there's no sails to make, but repairing awnings was the main thing. After some of these storms, they all needed repairing. A lot of my spare time was spent making a few leather handbags or trying to. I don't remember the petty officer that I was working with, but he was very, very good at this and he taught me quite a lot.

Many of the recently liberated areas of the Far East showed a distinct lack of enthusiasm at the prospect of becoming British colonies again and swapping one master for another. The late 1940s was thus still a fairly active period for the Pacific Fleet, which was itself struggling with the dramatic drop in manpower associated with demobilization.

Service in the Pacific entailed a couple of additional minor refits for *Belfast*, despite the comprehensive reworking she had undergone simply to get there. Lessons learned during the closing stages of the war were being rapidly applied. Nevertheless, a balance had to be struck between new equipment being taken on board and older equipment deemed less useful being removed to keep weight and stability within acceptable margins.

In February 1946 the depth charges were removed, albeit they'd always been something of a last-ditch resort. But the removal of the ship's torpedoes in Sydney robbed her of her biggest punch against ships larger than herself, although the tubes themselves were left in place in case they were needed again. This loss wasn't as bad as it might seem. With Japan, Germany, and Italy out of the picture as naval threats for a good time to come, the only nations left with functioning modern battleships were the United States, Great Britain, and France. Other nations either had no gun-based capital ships or else had command of obsolete vessels of World War I vintage in various stages of repair. While potential future enemies might possess cruisers in somewhat greater numbers, that was what the main battery was for.

After a general tour of the western Pacific, late spring and early summer of 1946 found the ship at Singapore, where additional work was done. More updates, reversion to peacetime conditions, and "tropicalising" prepared the ship for a planned extended deployment in the warmer reaches of the world.

The improvements included:

- A radar training suite to allow newly arrived crew to be brought up to speed while on deployment
- Improved air conditioning
- New showers
- Unsealing of scuttles blocked off during the war along with additional ones being installed in living quarters
- General improvements to living quarters
- Additional derrick cranes to facilitate reprovisioning the ship

Released from the dockyard in late July, *Belfast* now became the flagship of the Fifth Cruiser Squadron. She spent most of the rest of the year shuttling back and forth between China and Japan, engaged in efforts to maintain stability in the region. She spent a good portion of the first half of 1947 at or near Malaya, which was on something of a downward spiral that would eventually lead to the outbreak of a communist-backed insurgency.

By mid-1947 the further drawing down of the Royal Navy was in full swing. Despite her status as one of the least worn, largest, and most modernised cruisers in the fleet, *Belfast* was ordered home to be placed into the reserves. Britain was not alone in the postwar drawdowns. The Marine Nationale of France and the U.S. Navy were also in the middle of massive drawdowns as ships were being scrapped or mothballed in job lots. Some would have only a few years' rest before the Korean War and then the Cold War brought them back out onto the seas once more.

In the case of *Belfast*, the Royal Navy appreciated that she might be needed soon, and so the year in reserve was accompanied by maintenance on her machinery and yet another rearrangement of her lighter AA armament. As tensions continued to rise in the western Pacific, she was called back into service in late 1948. Before heading out she made a stopover in her namesake city, during which she acquired the solid silver bell that still adorns the quarterdeck.

> *George Moody:*
>
> *Belfast had just come home from a '46–'48 commission and she was recruiting to go back out again. So we got pulled into the Belfast, for a two-year trip out to the Far East.*

Belfast arrived in the Pacific in early 1949 and took up her old station in the Fifth Cruiser Squadron. The situation in the region had rapidly deteriorated, at least from the viewpoint of the Western Allies. The civil war in China was reaching its end-state, with the forces of soon-to-be-Chairman Mao in the ascendency. The ship was involved to one degree or another in a series of incidents. The first was the recovery of an RAF Vampire jet fighter that had been forced down by mechanical failure but ended up on a beach in territory held by the Communist Chinese. *Belfast* sailed into the bay in question to retrieve the jet. A landing party quickly got the aircraft out of the sand and onto a pontoon, and then towed the pontoon out to the cruiser, which

The space between the superstructure and fore funnel proved to be a useful storage area for the recovered Vampire jet fighter, which was returned to an Allied air base relatively swiftly without any of its secrets being exposed. (Imperial War Museum)

hauled the jet on board and took it back to friendly territory before communist forces could arrive.

Murray Ward:

I was drafted out to the Belfast. Every morning we reported to the officers of the barracks and they said two were going somewhere else and your number wasn't up that day. So then on the third day they said you're going to the Belfast on Friday. So I took passage out to Hong Kong, and from Hong Kong I took passage on the Unicorn, this aircraft carrier, that took six weeks. I thought we'd be away for about a year or so as that was [the] usual commission then. I joined the ship in Saigon; from Saigon we went to Singapore, Hong Kong.

The only good thing about the Belfast was the stokers' mess was on the upper deck, so you saw daylight all the time. It's not now, it's down below now they've converted it (the post-Korea modernisation), but back then it was on the upper deck.

After rescuing the Vampire, *Belfast* played something of a backseat role in the famous *Amethyst* incident, in which the sloop HMS *Amethyst* was attacked and disabled on the Yangtze River by the Communists' field-gun batteries. While it was *London*, *Consort*, *Concord*, and *Black Swan* that physically tried to reach and relieve *Amethyst*, as the flagship, *Belfast* had the peripheral role of coordinating the rescue efforts while keeping in contact with the stricken sloop and playing off the Communists' local field commander. *Amethyst* eventually escaped, and *Belfast* patrolled the mouth of the river for the next few weeks to make sure the situation didn't escalate.

George Moody:

As you know, the Amethyst incident happened and the London was fired upon, the Concord was fired on as well as the Amethyst. We were in Hong Kong at the time, and we embarked 300 British soldiers and went up to the Yangtze, went to a place called Alacrity Anchorage. We were there with a couple of destroyers, and these 300 soldiers were dispersed throughout the ship, so many in each mess. Well, we had three in No. 28 mess, and one incident happened one day [with] Able Seaman Murphy, who was in our mess, who loved his tot beyond anything; he had to have his rum. . . . This day we were just pouring the tots out when we decided to give these three soldiers a sip of each of our tots just so they didn't feel left out. Well, Murphy, he offered this soldier his tot, to have a sip. And the soldier, the soldier took it completely wrong way, not knowing what the tot meant or what it was, and downed the lot smooth as anything. Murphy's face went white, I would say ashen, never spoke a word, and just stormed out of the mess onto the upper deck, where he was pacing about like a man possessed. We then approached this soldier and said: "What did you do that for?"

He said, "Do what?"

"It's the way that you sipped, stupid."

He said, "Well, he gave me it."

"No, he meant you to have a sip of his tot like this."

We showed him then and he was full of remorse, but it was too late. We went and found Murphy and brought food back down off the upper deck and we made him a tot up out of our rum which calmed the situation somewhat. But not enough for Murphy ever to be friends with that soldier again.

Belfast also spent some time off Malaya, where the situation had degenerated into the full-scale Malayan Emergency while the ship had been in the reserves. But between this duty and visits to Japan and Hong Kong she was due back in Singapore by 1950 for another round of maintenance and refits. By this stage the equipment that increasingly cluttered her mast, superstructure, and upper deck areas was a cause for significant concern. Thus, apart from cleaning the hull and generally further improving her ability to handle tropical conditions, most of the other changes apart from the start of fitting Type 268 radar were removals or replacements as opposed to additions. This included:

- New fire control directors for some of the light AA guns
- Removal of old acoustic equipment
- Removal of some of the large signal lights
- Removal of a large optical rangefinder for the 6-inch battery, reflecting the ever-growing reliance on radar for gunnery control

Phillip Cookson:

Very, very, very impressive, she was much bigger [than his previous ship] and she had 12 6-inch guns rather than 9, which her people were keen to use to make her heard. And we were very impressed with her.

This work was completed by mid-spring 1950, but regular cruising lasted for only about six weeks before the Korean War broke out and *Belfast* was called upon to fight in her second war.

Murray Ward:

Then the Korean War broke out, so I did two years and ten months before we got out. We [were] supposed to be about a year but ended up spending two years and ten months with them.

Alan Doick:

But while I was in Hong Kong, the Korean War broke out and I was ashore. And the Mounts Bay [a frigate] went off to Korea. I went to Japan in an aircraft carrier to catch up with the ship. We got to Sasebo, I think it was, and rejoined Mounts Bay. And I remember going out on and training with the United Nations and there were loads of ships there, American ships, Australian, Indian, all sorts. And they put a plane and a drone over the fleet and the Americans were putting up so much barrage of flak the sky was black with the puffs of smoke, and the officers on our ship said, "Remember, this shell has cost a lot of money and the Chancellor (whoever it was at the time) can't afford to pay for them," so we were doing single shots, bang, bang, bang, and we shot down the drone. That was a good memory. And then at some point in Sasebo, I went on the Belfast. Which was a completely different experience because from a fairly small ship like a frigate it was a big ship at the time, although looking at it now, it doesn't seem all that big. But at the time it was. My first impressions were when late one afternoon I joined Belfast. Practically everybody was ashore and I thought, God, this is a big ship, and I got allocated a mess and joined it, met the lads, and I thought this is a ship that you could get lost in. It was a happy ship, the Belfast.

First of all, they put me in this 6-inch gun room down below and handling the cordite for the 6-inch guns, getting it ready to fire for when we went to battle stations; then they locked the hatch up and I thought, "Well, I don't like that because if anything happens, I'll be locked in here, I've got to transfer to a pom-pom," which was up on deck. That was fine and so I spent the Korean War on a pom-pom.

Often misattributed to D-Day, this photo shows *Belfast* bombarding enemy positions in Korea. The paint scheme is the most obvious indication of the era. (Imperial War Museum)

Belfast moored alongside U.S. Navy ships in a brief respite from patrolling the enemy coastline during the Korean War. (Imperial War Museum)

THE KOREAN WAR

When forces from Communist North Korea invaded South Korea, *Belfast* was hurriedly made ready for war and put to sea in the early morning hours. She met up with other ships of the British Pacific Fleet that were likewise sortieing before proceeding in force to Okinawa, where the U.S. Seventh Fleet was assembling. *Belfast* was carrying a peacetime crew, which meant there weren't enough men on board to man all the weapons. One of the main battery turrets and a good portion of the light antiaircraft weapons would have to be left unattended until more men could be brought out to her.

The crew was a mixture of new sailors who had joined the Navy in the past five years and longer-serving veterans. It fell to the latter to help the former quickly come to grips with the procedures of not just operating the ship but also preparing her for action.

They didn't have much time to accomplish that. In the very opening days of the conflict *Belfast* was part of the escort for the USS *Philippine Sea* as she launched air strikes. Within only a few days, however, it became clear that the North Korean navy was a far from formidable foe, and most of the fleet's cruisers were not needed in the aircraft carrier escort role.

So it came to pass that less than two weeks after the war had broken out, *Belfast*'s guns spoke once more—this time in support of the beleaguered South Korean forces—bombarding the advancing communist troops repeatedly. Occasionally these bombardments were self-directed, using the ship's own range-finding equipment, but more often they were long-range indirect bombardments, with the fall of shot called in by forward observers on the ground or by aircraft orbiting above the battlefield. Ironically, the ship's original complement of aircraft would have been well suited for that role; but in the event, liaison with the pilots and observers from other ships and services proved to not be difficult to work out.

Belfast **in the last peaceful days of 1950 before being drawn back into conflict. (Imperial War Museum)**

Phillip Cookson:

We went on to Okinawa and then we joined up with an American carrier group and we went to the east coast of Korea because the North had started invading. They were making quite good, good progress down there. We carried out a bombardment of these chaps, and it was the first time that the South Koreans counterattacked and regained some ground. So that was quite satisfactory.

Sidney Pickett:

[O]n patrol, as the admiral's yeoman I [was] stationed on the Admiral's Bridge, and the admiral would from time to time come up there and watch and see what's happening. I'd generally be stood next to him discussing if as I was a young person my eyesight was better than his as an elderly person. One of the things he was mainly observing is the bombardment. You could see the enemy shells coming our way, they splashed a long way before they got to us. We'd be touring up and down the west coast of Korea, a couple of times we went off to somewhere in South Korea and I went ashore with dispatches and things like that. I remember being entertained very well by the army.

The ability to call on what in army terms amounted to a battery and a half of heavy artillery (two batteries if the necessary additional crew could be found) anywhere within 13 miles (20 km) of the coast was critical for the survival of the Allied troops, who were at this stage being driven back by the North Koreans' offensive.

Within the Allied fleet, *Belfast* soon gained a reputation for fast and accurate shooting. She was also able to bring her 4-inch guns into play at closer ranges than larger ships could, and her gunners proved very adept at picking off enemy trains moving up and down the coast. Occasionally the 6-inch main battery was allowed to have some of the fun by using star shell instead to illuminate the target.

Apart from trains and troop concentrations, *Belfast*'s targets included radio stations, shore batteries, barracks, power stations, supply dumps, and the landscape itself, since it turned out that a good number of coastal roads and rail-lines were cut into the cliffs and hills and a judicious application of 6-inch shells at narrower stretches was capable of dropping whole sections of infrastructure into the sea or into the valley below. This was far more disruptive to enemy resupply efforts than taking out individual trains and truck convoys, because rebuilding the destroyed sections would require bridging as well as relaying works, and these efforts themselves could of course be targeted.

George Moody:

They kept us out there another six months; she saw quite a bit of action on her next voyage, after I left. But we did a couple of goals. The first place I remember was we were with the aircraft carrier Triumph. The war hadn't been started that long ago and we were patrolling off the east coast of Korea with the Triumph. There was a coastal road, and that was the first time we ever, on that commission, saw any action. Well, if you want to call it that, there were two or three tanks on the road and the Belfast fired a 4-inch just into the mountains to cause a landslide to block the road up. Then the Triumph sent planes out, they dropped napalm on them, which is now banned. Of course, we fired the 6-inch, the main armament, as well. They were firing at different targets inland, with planes spotting for them to see where the fall of the shot was, but we didn't see a lot of action. We did a lot of patrols around Korea but not so much action early on.

We were too close to the shore one night and a 40-mm, which is like a pom-pom or a Bofors, shell hit the mainmast. It didn't do a lot of damage and I think it only injured a couple of chaps. It was too close in shore, we shouldn't have been that close in. That's about the only thing that ever happened to us on that trip.

Murray Ward:

Once the war started, I was working on boats, the motorboats to take people ashore, and we carried a landing craft while we were off Korea. My job was looking after the engine on the landing craft. During the war we'd go ashore and pick wounded up and bring prisoners back and take some Marines ashore overnight . . . to test where they would bombard the next day. Most of the time we were taking Marines ashore, putting them ashore to find positions to bombard and radio back. We bombard and then the next night we go and pick them up. More rarely we'd pick prisoners up they'd caught, or pick wounded up because we had a hospital on board.

Soon *Belfast* had fired more shells off the coast of Korea than she had during the entirety of World War II, wear-

The cold Korean winters brought ice buildup again, although fortunately not to the extent experienced in the Arctic. (Imperial War Museum)

ing out the main guns and requiring a trip back to Singapore for replacements. Typically she would spend about four weeks on station with four days' relief at Sasebo before returning to action. By October 1950 it was clear that the war was not going to be over by Christmas, and *Belfast* was ordered back home to Chatham for a quick fortnight of work to allow her to go back to Korea for the long haul. This would include receiving additional crew to bring her up to her full complement so that all the main battery turrets could be fully manned consistently.

Phillip Cookson:

I was to be assigned to one of the pom-poms, 40-mm, either four-barrel ones or we had two eight-barrel ones as well. You're still responsible for seeing that the orders are carried out from the gun officer if something happened. You know, like an aircraft coming in on the starboard side or something like that. Then set the gun director on tracking and open fire if it was in range and what have you.

We didn't fire then in anger, maybe because we were too far off from the chaos. They certainly didn't send in the aircraft to hunt for us, although they didn't seem to like the Belfast so much, but it was sort of far out of town there. Probably quite sensible actually. I did get fired on later, which was not agreeable.

But while I was there nobody would dare shoot at Belfast. I think she was far too impressive. She seemed to have a charmed life like that. We did a lot of bombardment there, including the bombardment for the Inchon landings. Then after the one bombardment troops were landed and they virtually cut the peninsula in two, and it all looked as though the war was over and the North Koreans were in in full flight. So, at that time they said, "Right? War looks like it'll be over by October. We can send Belfast home now to recommission." Because that had been delayed. No sooner were we off station than the Chinese came into the war. They must've said, "It's all right now, Belfast's gone, we can go and take the rest of South Korea." So we raced home to Chatham, which is our home port, and we recommissioned there and then we came back, but we were off station, I suppose, for three months or something like that.

Murray Ward:

They came back to recommission in the middle of the war. Belfast went back to England and came back again after they changed crews. I stayed out there as well as all the admiral's staffers. The other staff stayed out there and the admiral as well, all on the Jamaica, Kenya, or the Sheffield. Then Belfast came back again but only two or three of crew that I knew came back with it, but not many. Those that did had joined just before I had, so they didn't do their two years yet, so they went home and came back with it. Then they came back with me when I came back in '52.

Between this working up and then physically getting back to the operational area, *Belfast* wasn't back on station until the end of January 1951. She arrived to find a situation rather different from the one she had left. The South Korean and UN forces had pushed back the North Koreans' advance, only to be pushed back in turn by China's dramatic intervention, which was now just about in the process of being itself checked, albeit with the front lines still well south of the 38th Parallel.

After her return to duty on the west coast of Korea *Belfast* conducted a mixture of bombardment missions similar to those she had undertaken in the past paired with newer mission profiles; general harassment of the enemy was now just as important. As a Tribal-class destroyer flotilla and the Polish *Piorun* had demonstrated against the *Bismarck* almost a decade earlier, keeping the enemy awake at night badly diminished their combat capability the next day, and sporadic nighttime flurries of shells could indirectly save as many or more lives than the deletion of a supply train or the destruction of a specific enemy troop concentration, especially as UN forces were advancing at this stage of the war, which meant any reduction of the defenders, capabilities was especially welcome.

The ship's main guns fire on enemy positions off the coast of Korea in 1951. (Imperial War Museum)

Phillip Cookson:

Well, when we returned we went back to the old sort of patrols and bombarding from time to time, helping the army with gunfire support for the troops. Our base was Sasebo, in Japan, an enormous number of ships of enormous number of different nations too. It's really quite interesting. And the Japanese? Looked after their ship's company very well.

Each patrol would last three weeks, something like that, but she could easily have stayed out longer than that. There's the clinician at sea and so on, lots of room for stores and what have you.

As an officer of quarters you were responsible for just that particular pom-pom gun. But the gunnery officer, of course, has overall control. And he will be told what you're supposed to be doing.

There would be dawn and dusk action stations, and then if you were going to do a bombardment, they would be going to action stations for that. But we didn't spend our whole time there. A lot of time you were just there as a deterrent to the enemy and to make it more unliveable for them in all ways, but really to support the army in particular if need be.

The weather proved to be a more difficult adversary than the Communists, at least as far as the ship was concerned. Gales and typhoons were bad enough, but the wild temperature fluctuations kept the men off balance as well. Even with the air conditioning, it could be a question of how much clothing a man could ditch before he either became indecent or an officer called him out for being out of uniform. In winter the ship forged through dangerous ice floes, and the fitting of steam-powered heating back in 1942 was much appreciated. It wasn't quite as bad as the Arctic ice had been, but it wasn't far removed. And in the middle of all this was the need to refuel and reprovision at sea.

Another new role was that of decoy. Along with other ships *Belfast* took part in fake advances and even entire faked amphibious landings to draw enemy troops away from the front lines. It took pressure off the troops on the ground while also affording the decoy forces a chance to take shots at enemy formations without having to worry about hitting the UN troops.

Aside from a brief respite in June 1951 for a quick refit that revealed some issues with her machinery, *Belfast* was otherwise almost always on station, with her time split roughly two to one between the west and east coasts of Korea. Her association with aircraft salvage operations came to the fore again during this period when a MiG-15 jet fighter crashed in shallow water off the west coast. While *Belfast* was not expected to haul away this particular wreck—that honour going to an LSV more suited to the shoals in the area—she was on hand at the edge of the deeper water to provide antiaircraft cover should the operation come under attack or the North Koreans attempt to bomb the aircraft to deny it to the Allies. In the event, the enemy appeared unaware of what had happened, and the MiG-15 was soon on its way for dissection.

The *Belfast* was assigned to a number of different formations after that, briefly working in conjunction with the battleship USS *New Jersey* (also now a museum ship) and later as part of TG95.8 as the flagship trying to make sense of the combined British, Australian, American, Dutch, and Canadian forces assigned to it. The carrier HMAS *Sydney* provided air spotting to the rest of the formation as well as launching her own bombing missions, with the cruisers and destroyers in turn providing suppression barrages when the aircraft went in to keep enemy AA gun crews in cover.

The end of November saw her first extended break of the year with successive port visits to Yokosuka, Japan, and Hong Kong before arriving back on station two days before Christmas. Christmas and New Year's Day were celebrated in part by targeting the hated Amgak batteries, a set of combined artillery and antiaircraft installations that menaced both shipping and pilots at irregular intervals. The Allied forces' coastal blockade was also slotted into *Belfast*'s roles, as well as supporting behind-the-lines operations with gunfire when needed.

This state of affairs characterised most of 1952, which also saw the only combat-related casualties of the war for the ship when in July a 76-mm shell from a shore battery that *Belfast* was attacking scored a hit on the forward part of the ship, killing one and wounding four others—all Chinese ratings.

The war ended in late September, and *Belfast* handed off her position to HMS *Newcastle*. She headed back to Britain, where she was sent into Class III reserve by the end of the year.

Alan Doick:

I remember a shell hit. They had guns or mortar guns on rails in Korea and they used to quickly bring them out of the cliff on the rails and fire a shot and go back in again. So by the time the ship got the binoculars on, trained round the guns, and so on, they door had disappeared. Belfast was hit on a starboard side, as I recall it, by such a gun. It came in at the stewards' mess. But I don't remember firing back; I don't think we did.

We used to lay down loads of explosives with the bigger guns, the 4-inch and 6-inch; the smaller ones weren't involved very much. That was a time an American plane came over; we were sailing up and it shouldn't have been there, and I opened fire and fortunately I didn't bring it down because they were so quick in those days. Well, they're a lot quicker now, of course.

Belfast alongside USS _Bataan_ off the Korean coast in May 1952. (NHHC)

When *Belfast* was commissioned she carried a biplane. After years without aircraft, by the 1950s she was regularly hosting helicopters. (Imperial War Museum)

RESERVES AND MODERNISATION

Belfast's fate was somewhat undecided at this stage. Although she remained one of the Royal Navy's largest and most up-to-date cruisers, she also required a larger crew, which was expensive. Further, there were some cruisers either in service or about to enter service that had even fewer hours on their hulls and were also smaller. While this generally left them far less capable in an actual fight, they were cheaper to run, and that appealed greatly to those who commanded desks in Whitehall. A few sketches were made of proposed updates, but these then went into abeyance for a couple of years as arguments over cost and the extent of the modernisation boiled away in the background.

Bizarrely, in some ways it was the Soviet Union that saved her. The Soviets had continued to build their fleet of cruisers, especially the *Sverdlov* class, and the Western Allies deemed some kind of cruiser-killing force necessary for the foreseeable future. By early 1955 this looked like it was going to be the battleship HMS *Vanguard*, then in refit, but after a change in government it was decided to keep two additional cruisers in the fleet for this role instead.

The issue was cost. While anyone with even a modicum of sense had to recognize that *Vanguard* was infinitely more capable of dealing with one or more *Sverdlovs* than *Belfast*, let alone any of the other cruisers in the Royal Navy at the time, the battleship was considerably larger, and thus on paper the amount of money needed to keep her in commission was larger than that needed for any cruiser. That the manpower and maintenance costs of keeping two cruisers in commission were actually greater is the kind of minor detail that rarely bothers politicians who aim for a

TABLE 14.1. SPECIFICATIONS OF *VANGUARD*, *BELFAST*, AND *SVERDLOV*

	HMS *Vanguard*	HMS *Belfast*	*Sverdlov*
Displacement (standard/deep)	44,500 tons/51,420 tons	c. 11,500 tons/14,500 tons	13,600 tons/16,640 tons
Main battery	8 x 15-inch (4 twin turrets)	12 x 6-inch (4 triple turrets)	12 x 6-inch (4 triple turrets)
Effective battle range	30,000 yards/17 miles	22,000 yards/12.5 miles	25,000 yards/14 miles
Speed	30 knots	32 knots	32.5 knots
Belt armour	14-inch	4.5-inch	3.9-inch
Deck armour	6-inch	3-inch (over magazines)	2-inch
Crew	c. 15-1600 (post removal of 40-mm Bofors)	c. 880	c. 1,250

quick headline while praying no one bothers with any particularly deep analysis.

In light of this and other decisions made regarding the cruiser fleet, *Belfast* was earmarked for modernization in early 1955, with the work itself scheduled to be undertaken in 1956 when she was due for a scheduled refit anyway, which now would be significantly extended. This would be the most comprehensive reworking of the ship, surpassing even her refit after her encounter with the mine near the start of her service career.

The reconfiguration was in part driven by the changing nature of anticipated battlefields. The new *Belfast* would be able to fight in what we today call NBC (Nuclear, Biological, Chemical) conditions but back then was referred to as ABCD (Atomic, Biological, and Chemical Warfare Defence). Not only did the ship's citadel and forward superstructure have to be able to be made airtight, they would also need to operate at a slight positive pressure so that any leaks or battle damage would not allow contaminants easy admission into the ship's ventilation and circulation systems.

So, the old cylindrical superstructure, a hallmark of the Town class, had to go. In its place came a larger structure with six flat sides somewhat reminiscent of the "Queen Anne's Mansion" style found on British battleships since the launch of the *Nelson* class. While it was not everyone's favourite choice, aesthetically it remains—in the author's opinion, at least—somewhat

HMS *Vanguard* was without question a better counter to the USSR's *Sverdlovs*. In an alternate timeline she might be sitting on the Thames instead of *Belfast*. (NHHC)

better than the "cube" setup that was beginning to gain popularity and could be seen to eye-watering effect on the soon-to-be-completed HMS *Tiger*, then in the final stages of fitting out. The new superstructure had room for a full Admiral's Bridge in additional to the regular bridge, to be fitted alongside an Operations Room, better known in the United States as a combat information center (CIC), along with other needed facilities—all inside the sealed environment. A concession to British captains' habit of commanding their ships in the open air was made in the form of a minimally equipped command area atop the new superstructure from which the ship could be commanded in peacetime and/or fair weather.

Most of the major bulkheads were fully sealed to improve survivability, a feature that means visitors to the ship today must ascend and descend several decks repeatedly to visit lower areas of the ship such as the magazines and machinery areas. A system for damping down the superstructure ahead of a nuclear strike was installed to minimize the impact of fallout, along with dedicated decontamination departments, more emergency lighting, and the ability to rapidly blank off the ship's scuttles, which had previously required dockyard work to accomplish.

The increasingly laden tripod masts were replaced wholesale with square-cross-section lattice masts configured to support the ship's various radars and other electronic equipment. Most of the timber decking was removed as a possible fire or contamination hazard and replaced with anti-slip paint. It could only be hoped that the heating and cooling systems would be able to keep up with the fluctuating temperatures inside the ship that would result from the loss of the insulation provided by the decking. If those systems failed, then the common sailor would have to hope their Lordships in the Admiralty saw fit to assign *Belfast* to a temperate climate.

The ship's main armament would remain the same. Unlike many World War II–era vessels, thanks to care taken in previous refits plus the work done in her reconstruction she did not need to lose a main battery turret to make room for her other equipment. Her fire control equipment was significantly updated, though; this included new or replacement equipment for the 6-inch, 4-inch, and 40-mm batteries.

The 40-mm armament was also completely reworked. The mix of various Bofors mountings along with pom-poms was completely removed and replaced by six twin Mk V Bofors mounts, two on each bridge wing, for a total of four and two aft, one each side of the aft superstructure. A new sonar system, at this stage still called Asdic in British parlance, was installed, and the final remnants of the depth charge equipment as well as the torpedo tubes and their control systems were removed.

Navigation equipment was updated, machinery was repaired, and water and refrigeration systems were improved, although the electrical system remained DC. Aircraft made a surprise return to the ship as the quarterdeck was made capable of receiving helicopters—as long as someone remembered to train the aftmost gun turret, Y, over to one side to get the gun barrels out of the way. Remote control positions for the machinery were also installed to allow the boilers and engines to be operated indirectly.

The new masts and superstructure supported a wide variety of aerials, but the main radar in place was now:

- Type 262 for close-range gunnery
- Type 274 for the main battery at longer ranges
- Type 277Q for altitude determination and as a surface search radar
- Type 293Q, which did the same as 277Q but at closer ranges
- Type 960M air search radar
- Type 974 for dedicated surface search at range

Desired items envisaged before dockyard capacity and cost-cutting took them away included:

- A more sophisticated fire control system for the 4-inch battery, which was deleted because of the requirement for more rewiring and a lot of work below deck compared with the "drop-in" nature of the system actually installed
- More 40-mm Bofors installations
- The reintroduction of the two aft 4-inch twin mounts
- "CAMROSE" rocket-propelled antitorpedo torpedoes, which were dropped because the program was cancelled around the time the refit finally got under way

Despite these and a few other limitations, *Belfast* still emerged with as advanced a system setup as any ship

Belfast's new configuration features a lattice mast and an angular superstructure. More accurate but fewer antiaircraft guns and other new features allowed reduction of the old tripod mast. (Author's collection)

in the Royal Navy. Further, her displacement was actually reduced by a few hundred tons and her stability improved by a fair degree as a result.

Recommissioning on 12 May 1959, *Belfast* continued working up while making her way gradually east, arriving at Singapore in December of the same year. The coming year, 1960, looked to be somewhat interesting. Although the Korean War had officially been in abeyance for some time, tensions were still high, and SEATO (South East Asia Treaty Organization), the local version of NATO, was looking to put on a major exercise, codenamed Sealion, in the spring.

Sealion was a considerable undertaking involving more than 60 ships from Australia, New Zealand, the United States, the United Kingdom, France, India, the Philippines, Thailand, and Pakistan. *Belfast* was at the heart of the action, at one point sailing alongside the carriers USS *Yorktown*, HMS *Albion*, and HMAS *Melbourne*. The American and Australian carriers led two task groups while *Belfast* was flagship of the third. The exercise included simulated air attacks courtesy of the carriers' air wings and antisubmarine warfare (ASW) exercises in which U.S. Seventh Fleet submarines simulated attacks on *Melbourne*.

Although the exercises were simulations, they took place in a tense atmosphere. Even before the exercise began, many ships were running at action stations when passing through areas where North Korean or other communist vessels might be encountered. Sealion included visits to Seoul and Inchon, and the exercise appears to have served its purpose in deterring any renewal of hostilities.

Belfast rounded out the year docked in Singapore as most of the crew headed home by air, to be replaced by others flying in. However, her active service life was coming to a close. On 31 January 1961 she began her last overseas commission. She soon found herself back in the business of crashed aircraft when a Sea Vixen from HMS *Hermes* that she was tracking smashed into the sea 20 miles away. She proceeded at speed to the crash site, and at first the situation didn't look good. An oil slick and wreckage were the only things the ship's whaler found. But soon orbiting aircraft pointed them to survival dinghies a little farther away, where they found the aircraft's crew bobbing about awaiting rescue.

Then it was on to Exercise JET '61 (24 February–10 March 1961). Reprising her first ever assignment, *Belfast* played the part of commerce raider and adopted a somewhat questionable disguise as an oil tanker. The advances of technology since 1939 became clear when she was discovered shortly into the exercise by a flight of Venom jet fighters from the Australian carrier *Melbourne*.

Belfast **undergoing reconstruction in 1958. Note how high in the water she sits, indicating that many systems have yet to be reinstalled in addition to the still-incomplete superstructure. (Author's collection)**

TABLE 14.2. RADAR AND RELATED ELECTRONIC SYSTEMS INSTALLED ON HMS *BELFAST*

Designation	Type	Notes
Type 242	IFF system for aircraft	An early IFF system fitted to the ship in 1942, worked alongside the Type 281 and removed with Type 281 in 1958/59 refit
Type 243	IFF system for aircraft	Newer IFF system installed in 1945 and still present on the ship
Type 251	IFF for ships	Installed in 1942 and still present on the ship
Type 252	IFF for ships	Worked alongside Type 273 and removed in the 1945 refit
Type 253	IFF for ships	Installed in 1945 and removed in 1959
Type 262	Close range gunnery control	Advanced postwar 30kW X-Band radar system installed in 1958/59 refit and still present on the ship, maximum range 29 nm (54 km)
Type 268	4-inch AA search and direction	Postwar 30kW X-Band radar installed in March 1950 and still present on the ship, maximum range 30 nm (55 km)
Type 273	Surface search and target indication	Common British WW2 100kW S-Band radar set, removed in 1945 in favour of Type 277, max range 23 nm (42 km)
Type 274	6-inch gunnery control	More advanced than Type 284, a 400kW F-Band radar that replaced the Type 284 on the ship in the 1945 refit, still present on the ship, max range 16 nm (30 km)
Type 277Q	Surface/air search and altitude finding	More advanced that Type 281, a 400kW S-Band radar that operated alongside the older radar after 1945, max range 11 nm (20 km)
Type 281	Air search	Second-generation HF-Band British radar, remained on the ship from 1942 to 1959, 70kW power and 100-nm (185-km) range in basic form and 350kW power and 120-nm (222-km) range in Type 281B form.
Type 282	Pom-pom direction	UHF-Band 25kW radar installed along with power control to the pom-poms in 1945, removed with the pom-poms in 1959, max range 3.5 nm (6.5 km)
Type 283	Blind barrage heavy AA	UHF-Band 25kW radar installed during the 1942 refit and removed in the final modernisation in 1959, max range 8.5 nm (16 km)
Type 284	6-inch gunnery control	Early UHF-Band 25–150kW (Type 284, 284M and 284P versions) gunnery control radar installed in 1942 and replaced by Type 274 in 1945, max range 10 nm (19 km) for basic Type 284
Type 285	AA control and direction	UHF-Band 25kW radar adapted from Type 284 for AA work, fitted in 1942 and only removed in 1959, guided the 4-inch until superseded by Type 268, max range 8.5 nm (16 km)
Type 293Q	Close range air and surface search	S-Band 500kW radar installed in 1945 and still present on the ship, max range 25 nm (46 km)
Type 960M	Air search	VHF-Band 450kW Cold War–era radar fitted in 1959 and still present on the ship, max range 175 nm (324 km)
Type 974	Surface search and navigation	Cold War–era 7kW X-Band radar fitted in 1959 and still present on the ship, max range 25 nm (46 km)

This was followed by another SEATO exercise, Pony Express (22 April–4 May 1961), which focused on large-scale amphibious landings. Although *Belfast* was assigned to a shore bombardment group, her helicopter pad saw much activity. At one stage she accompanied a frigate to look for the wreckage of yet another aircraft, a Scimitar from HMS *Victorious* that had crashed during the exercise. This time there would be no recovery of wreckage. The divers dispatched to investigate reported an unhealthy number of sharks in the water that had presumably also come to see what was going on in their patch of ocean.

This done and a rather large typhoon endured, the ship began a tour that included Hong Kong, Nagasaki, Kure, Hiroshima, and Tokyo. The crew enjoyed the luxuries of multiple periods of shore leave and engaged in a number of charitable exercises. The captain amused himself and the crew by designing and commissioning an antishark net that allowed the men to swim in relative safety when the ship was at anchor, albeit the jury-rigged nature of the device led some to question if it was truly shark-proof or merely the first course in a shark buffet. In any case, the net would give everyone a chance to get out of the water as the sharks devoured it, the mess being divided on whether or not sharks found cork floats particularly appetizing.

In July, the ship was in the process of preparing for overhaul at Singapore when word came that Iraq was saber-rattling in the direction of the recently independent Kuwait. *Belfast* was rapidly turned around to be ready to sail as other active units of the fleet headed west. The situation resolved itself a few days later, and the ship went in for a three-week period in drydock on schedule. She was back at sea in early August.

Belfast spent the latter part of 1961 on a cruise around Australia, engaging in at-sea exercises, and then crossing the Indian Ocean. The ship's company was present to witness the independence of Tanzania, with the ceremony overseen by HRH the Duke of Edinburgh, who dined on board the ship afterward. After that august occasion the ship returned to her normal stalking grounds. As 1961 turned into 1962, *Belfast* took part in JET '62, an exercise that included simulated atomic attacks along with the usual surface, subsurface, and airborne activities.

And then it was time to turn for home. She went the long way around, via Guam and Pearl Harbor, where the ship's company paid their respects to the USS *Arizona* before proceeding onward to San Francisco. Calls at Seattle and the three main ports of British Columbia followed.

Belfast **demonstrates a number of her Cold War features in Devonport in June 1959, including the prominent C35 hull number. (Author's collection)**

The ship was not attempting the Northwest Passage but simply using the voyage as a chance to perform a series of goodwill visits. After leaving Canadian waters she turned about and headed for Panama, making the transit through the canal on 3 June 1962 before heading for Trinidad. After the crew enjoyed a few days' leave the ship struck out across the Atlantic for home. She arrived ahead of schedule, because shortly after she commenced this leg of the voyage a crewman came down with appendicitis. Although the ship's onboard medical staff dealt with the emergency, standard policy was to increase speed to minimize the time before the ship was in range of land-based hospitals in case complications arose.

She arrived off Spithead on 19 June and hoisted her paying-off pennant, her last overseas commission concluded.

Belfast moors in Vancouver in May 1962 on her way back across the globe to the United Kingdom, returning home from the Pacific one last time. (Courtesy City of Vancouver)

At that point most of the crew were still unaware that their beloved ship had been on the brink of losing her visual identity while they were making their way around the world. Much as these days the buzzwords "stealth" and "drone" are fitted into almost any new naval project to make it seem up-to-date, in the late 1950s and early 1960s "helicopter" and "amphibious" showed up with distressing regularity. The helicopter was certainly coming into its own at this time, rapidly becoming established as useful for everything from plane guard duty for carriers to ASW warfare and rapid troop transport in amphibious operations as newer and more capable models were being introduced.

The problem was where to put them. Most navies were still operating fleets largely comprising designs that either predated World War II or were wartime construction. Many of these ships, from cruiser size and up, had at some point operated aircraft but had seen these facilities removed as radar took over functions seaplanes and flying boats had previously performed. But bringing helicopters on board was not as simple as just reinstating these facilities, because many of them had been amidships and used catapult launches and crane-controlled recoveries. A helicopter's vertical takeoff and landing capability was ill-suited to navigating through the superstructure of a moving ship. Some ships had mounted their aircraft fore or aft, and where that arrangement had existed the conversion to allow at least limited helicopter use was somewhat easier. Postwar naval construction had been relatively limited because of the glut of wartime ships,

Belfast at sea in June 1959, freshly recommissioned and largely in the condition she is in today as a museum. (Author's collection)

and most of these newer-built craft were too small to accommodate helicopters at all.

There was, of course, the option to convert existing aircraft carriers of various sizes into helicopter carriers, especially since a number of these ships were beginning to struggle with the size and weight of modern jet aircraft; but a carrier of any appreciable size and capacity was quite expensive to run. Thus, even navies that could do this, mainly the U.S. Navy and the Royal Navy, could maintain only a few such vessels. Smaller navies either had to come up with another solution or forfeit any significant helicopter capacity. The solution, it seemed, was the hybrid helicopter-cruiser. That in itself was not an entirely new concept; hybrid aviation-capable cruisers such as the Swedish *Gotland* and the Japanese *Oyodo* had been designed and built prior to and during World War II, along with dubiously useful conversions such as the Japanese *Mogami*.

In the era of early missile technology, the cruiser hull seemed to offer an all-in-one package: large enough to support a number of helicopters aft while retaining either a gun or missile armament (or possibly both) amidships and forward that would make the ship a self-escorting jack-of-all-trades. Some converted or purpose-built ships were eventually used in this role—the aesthetic tragedy that would befall HMS *Tiger* and *Blake* late in the 1960s being an example—but at the turn of the decade the Royal Navy was looking at its older ships. Aside from the fact that a cruiser was cheaper to run than a carrier, the navy needed something to show for the rather embarrassing debacle of HMS *Swiftsure*, whose refit had been stopped partway through while schemes to turn her from a gun-based cruiser to a Land Craft (Assault) (LCA) carrier were considered. But converting the small *Minotaur*-class cruiser into a helicopter carrier would have produced a vessel that could take perhaps a bit more than half a squadron at a cost that could pay for the conversion of all three *Centaur*-class aircraft carriers to the same role, and the latter ships could support three to four times as many helicopters each. In the end, *Swiftsure* was sold to the scrappers in 1962.

With the long-delayed *Tiger* class about to enter service, and still some years away from two of them being burdened with the giant boxes that characterized this sort of conversion, the Royal Navy thought *Belfast* was about to become redundant. Since she would be replaced on frontline duty by these "new" ships, why

Belfast flying all her flags in May 1959, most likely for a Navy Day put on for the civilians touring the ship. (Author's collection)

not use her as a helicopter cruiser? She was, after all, somewhat larger than *Swiftsure* and could have more potential as a conversion.

The first conversion plan was quite basic: the removal of Y turret (the aftmost), along with much of the aft superstructure, to accommodate four LCAs on davits, two companies of troops, and as many Wessex helicopters as could be made to fit in the resulting space on the quarterdeck. Quite what the bemused crew of X turret were supposed to be doing in this situation—apart from ruining everyone's hearing and breaking expensive helicopters every time they fired—remains unstated.

Then someone realized that the ship didn't have the space to accommodate the approximately 350 additional men who would be coming on board without cutting into the remaining ship's crew. The ship's speed would have to be reduced as a result, because there would be only enough engineering-qualified men to run one of the boilers. Further, there would be only enough gunners to man the AA batteries and one gun turret—which at least answered what X turret would be doing: most likely nothing except perhaps serving as a heavily armed tearoom for the pilots.

These considerations led to some attempts at rationalizing the plan, which was advanced to remove both X and Y turrets, plus all superstructure aft of the second funnel down to the level of X turret. A flight deck would then be extended out at this level with accommodation built beneath it and a hangar constructed that would run from just forward of the previous position of X turret right up to the back of the second funnel.

Most of the ship's antiaircraft armament and fire control directors would be removed to make room for the four LCAs and up to six Wessex helicopters, four in the hangar and two on the flight deck, leaving the ship with one working boiler room, the forward gun turrets, and the bridge wing 40-mm Bofors mounts operational.

While the total conversion cost was only about 20 percent of what had been estimated for *Swiftsure* while granting roughly the same maximum helicopter capacity and the ability to provide at least some fire support for the troops, it would also take about a year to accomplish, which was much too long. Every attempt to reduce the time needed by reducing the number of changes resulted in a proposal that lost a lot of capability and gained very little in return. With *Belfast* still en route toward home, her company blissfully unaware of the machinations aimed toward changing her into a completely different ship, the idea was quietly dropped, although some of the considerations from the project may have been used as the basis for the work done to two of the *Tigers* later in the same decade.

The once-elegant lines of the *Tiger*-class cruiser HMS *Blake* were ruined by the imposition of a large helicopter hangar aft. The hangar proposed for *Belfast* was even larger, roughly twice the overall volume being dedicated to flight facilities. (U.S. Navy)

Belfast had a remarkably quick turnaround, paying off fully on 2 July 1962 and recommissioning with a new crew later the same day. This commission was for Home Sea Service and entailed about seven months of touring U.K. and northern European ports before paying off into reserves at the end of January 1963. This was her last cruise with a full-time Royal Navy crew.

Michael Lumby:

I was in command of Belfast for about two or three months' time to do a cruise around Britain and come back to Plymouth. Well, somebody came and relieved me and did the spring cruise and then I think she was laid up. She'd just come back from China, she was very bright and she looked beautiful. She had lots of men on board who had kept her immaculate, certainly above the waterline. She was less so below the waterline. I was rather disappointed, I didn't think she was quite so smart down there as my old Bermuda. No problems, just not very clean; out of sight out of mind, I think.

When I had taken over I'd only just got into my cabin when police arrived and they wished to search my bathroom outside.

"Please do," I said. "What are we looking for?"

"We want to search," they said. "We have to take the panelling down."

I said, "Well, what? Tell me what you're looking for."

"We've had a message saying that the ship came back from China with drugs on board and they were hidden in the captain's bathroom."

They took the bathroom to pieces but never found any drugs. Somebody put the bathroom together again, which was nice.

Belfast's very last commission came later that year and lasted five weeks. Crewed by men of the Royal Navy Reserve and about 300 cadets, she spent most of this time in the Mediterranean as part of Exercise Rockhaul, in which she operated alongside a minesweeping flotilla and undertook communications drills and general fleet-related operations. It was hoped at the time that this cruise would become an annual event, as both RNR and cadet forces reported it a great success. But at least for the ship it was not to be. *Belfast* returned to Devonport on 24 August 1963 and paid off into reserves one last time.

***Belfast* in her final operational configuration just before she paid off in 1962. (Author's collection)**

RESERVES AND RESCUE

After her final payoff *Belfast* entered a career path familiar to hundreds of Royal Navy ships. The navy would find various uses for her, those usually involving replacing an older ship that was too worn out to continue in service. She would gradually deteriorate and be moved down in reserve categories until she was no longer worth reviving, and then it would be time for one last voyage to the scrappers.

Belfast **in final form was an imposing sight, but her time on the front lines was past. Fortunately, she survived long enough and in good enough condition to attract interest as a possible museum ship. (Imperial War Museum)**

Starting in 1965 she was utilized to beef up the numbers on a variety of Navy Days. Such service had two benefits. First, her participation gave the public a relatively large ship to tour. Aside from its aircraft carriers the Royal Navy by this point largely comprised destroyers and frigates, of which the very largest, the then-new County class, were barely more than half *Belfast*'s displacement. Second, it meant an active-duty warship could be kept out on station instead of being recalled for the event. That was important for the 1960s fleet, which had suffered a colossal reduction in hull numbers after various government budget cuts and botched programs saw many older ships leave service without any form of replacement.

She was then moved from Plymouth to Portsmouth for use as the accommodation vessel for the men who maintained the Reserve Ships Division based there. This role lasted from 1966 to 1970. In May 1971 came the inevitable notification that she had been "Reduced to Disposal." Her half-sister HMS *Sheffield*, which had been with *Belfast* at the Battle of North Cape and taken part in the hunt for *Bismarck*, had already suffered that fate. Even though *Sheffield* retained significantly more of her World War II character than the extensively refitted *Belfast*, her level of deterioration was such that preserving her as a museum would involve a huge expenditure of funds, and she had gone to the breakers in 1967.

Belfast, along with her smaller descendant *Gambia*, was still moored in Portsmouth as the 1970s dawned. Fortunately, she had survived long enough past her heyday to be considered "old"—or to be more polite, "historical"—and she came to the attention of people who had been working to try and preserve some element of the Royal Navy's World War II history. Somewhat characteristically for the United Kingdom, it was very much a last-minute affair. Students of history will recall that Nelson's flagship at Trafalgar, the first rate HMS *Victory*, was on the verge of rotting out and sinking or being broken up in the early 1920s when King George V stepped in and ensured her preservation within line of sight of *Belfast*'s then-current position in Fareham Creek.

The Imperial War Museum (Imperial War Museum) had managed to acquire and install a pair of 15-inch guns, all that was left of the dozens from Royal Navy dreadnought battleships, outside its Lambeth site in south London. In 1967 the staff had thought it would be a good idea to also preserve an entire turret. The largest turret still available was the triple 6-inch turret mounted on *Gambia*. They went to take a look, thinking only to acquire the turret, but on seeing the two once-proud ships moored up, someone had a brilliant idea. Why not try and preserve an entire warship instead?

But there was a problem with *Gambia*. Like *Sheffield* and many of the other older ships in the Reserve Fleet, she had been largely left to rot and had deteriorated to the point where turning her into a museum would require a lengthy and extensive overhaul. *Belfast*, on the other hand, was being used as the accommodation ship for the Reserves and had recently been in commission. The Reserve Fleet personnel had kept her watertight and her systems functional far more than the other ships under their care because they had to live on her. After a visit on board, the IWM staff concluded that *Belfast* would be the best candidate for preservation since she would require little work to be converted into a museum ship. A joint committee formed with the Ministry of Defence and the National Maritime Museum confirmed that converting her to a museum would be both practical and economical to carry out.

The matter should have been settled then and there. But in the great tradition of government bureaucracy, once presented with a feasible economic and cultural plan that would both preserve history and return a decent amount of money on a relatively small investment, the politicians decided that it was entirely too sane and sensible an idea. They rejected the proposal, preferring instead to issue the aforementioned notice of disposal to reclaim a pittance immediately from the scrap-metal merchants.

Luckily, all was not lost. *Belfast*'s last captain when she had been stationed overseas, Captain Morgan Charles Morgan-Giles, had since attained the rank of rear admiral, retired from the Royal Navy, and had become a Member of Parliament. With fond memories of his old ship and a voice that could be raised without violating the de facto arrangement that (ex)members of the armed forces did not comment directly on political matters, he was able to spearhead calls for the ship's preservation at the highest levels while also becoming the chairman of the HMS *Belfast* Trust, which had been established for the purpose of keeping the ship alive.

Faced with public embarrassment and unable to ignore the situation, the government gave in while also claiming credit for the idea. Thus, in July 1971, a scarce two months after her disposal had been ordered, HMS *Belfast* was formally transferred to the HMS *Belfast* Trust. In August the plans for her long-term future were announced. She was to be towed up the Channel to the Thames Estuary and from there up the river into the heart of London; she would pass through the famous Tower Bridge and on into the London Pool, the highest point up the river where large ships can moor. A special berth would be dredged there so that she wouldn't ground at low tide. She left Portsmouth on 1 September and reached Tilbury on the third, then spent the next month and a half having the needed work done to turn her from a reserve warship to a preserved museum ship. On 14 October she was released for the last leg of the trip to her new home. On Trafalgar Day, 21 October 1971, the First Sea Lord and the Minister for the Navy handed over the ship's White Ensign, which was then hoisted from the ensign staff on the quarterdeck by special dispensation. She had served the Royal Navy for 32 years, and at the time of this writing, has served the nation she once protected for another 53 years as a memorial and museum.

***Belfast*, moored in the upper reaches of Portsmouth as the accommodation ship for the Royal Navy Reserve Fleet, was a familiar sight to naval and civilian boats that sailed nearby. (Imperial War Museum)**

PRESERVATION

Belfast's story continues. Time and tide as well as visitors have taken a toll on the ship, as they do on any museum ship, while work has continued to enhance her as an attraction for visitors. The latter includes everything from supplying imitation foods for the ship's bakery, NAAFI (an onboard shop for the purchase of "luxury" items like chocolate), and mess areas, to restoring and fitting out the machinery spaces and parts of the forward superstructure. The Operations Room and Admiral's Bridge had been partially or fully stripped during the ship's time in the Reserves, so restoration involved a nationwide

Back in drydock again, *Belfast* is being prepared for her new life as a museum ship. (Imperial War Museum)

treasure hunt for parts either sold into private hands or identical components now held in Royal Navy stores—or else taken from other ships in the process of being brought into the Reserves or scrapped.

The ship's 40-mm Bofors mounts and their fire control directors were replaced three years after she opened to the public. All of this work and more, plus the upcoming need to drydock the ship for a more thorough overhaul, ate into the finances of the *Belfast* Trust, which was supported only by ticket sales and the occasional donation. In 1978 the Trust was merged with the IWM, which had recently expanded from Lambeth to include the air museum at Duxford. This merger went a long way to secure the ship's future. Her first drydocking as a museum ship occurred at Tilbury in 1982, with another in 1999 at Portsmouth.

When *Belfast* originally opened in 1971, only the upper decks and forward superstructure were accessible to the public. Additional areas have been opened since then, including the aforementioned machinery spaces and Ops Room, A and Y turrets, A and B shell rooms (but not the cordite magazines), the machine shop, the forward steering compartment, the fire control center, and various elements of the crew's accommodation, among others. More recent additions have included a café and the conversion of several unused compartments into interactive history exhibits, and the *World of Warships* gaming room, where visitors can take digital versions of *Belfast* in her 1943 and 1955 configurations into battle.

The mostly uniform blue-gray paint scheme—in which the author first saw her—remained until the 1999 drydocking. During that refit the ship was repainted to Admiralty Disruptive Camouflage Type 25, which she had worn from late 1942 through her engagement with *Scharnhorst* and the D-Day landings, and up until she was refitted for Pacific service.

While the Type 25 scheme leaves the ship in a slightly ahistorical position, because all other aspects of her appearance are that of her NBC-rated Cold War refit, a museum ship that spans multiple eras must be allowed some inconsistencies. The interactive onboard displays have also been updated over the past decade. In addition to informing the public about the ship's more famous World War II episodes, they now include her service in Korea and her other postwar adventures.

The last major physical changes to the ship took place in 2010, when a group of Russian businesses collaborated to manufacture lattice masts to replace the originals, which were rusting out. The new masts were built and installed as a mark of gratitude for *Belfast*'s role in the Arctic convoys that brought crucial supplies to the beleaguered Soviets.

Museum ships are generally held to require drydocking every couple of decades to maintain the best balance between cost and preservation,

Belfast **as she is today, moored in the London Pool just downstream of London Bridge. (Author's collection)**

but during the COVID-19 lockdown at the start of the 2020s the ship underwent an extensive internal renovation before reopening to the public in July 2021. It remains to be seen if *Belfast* will head to the drydock at some point in the 2020s, but for now she can still be visited where she first opened to the public more than half a century ago, her forward guns aimed at the former Scratchwood Services (now ambitiously renamed "London Gateway"), which Londoners sometimes joke indicates her readiness to "cause several million pounds of improvement at a moment's notice."

> *Murray Ward:*
> *They fired the guns on Belfast for the 50th and the 65th birthday. Did you know that? Only blanks, mind you, otherwise we would have killed half of London.*
>
> *John Harrison:*
> *There are the sort of ships such as, soon as you go on and you meet the crew, you know you're gonna be happy about that. Belfast was like that. It was. It was like joining a big group of friends. You knew you didn't know anybody, but they were immediately friends. It was a happy ship from the word go. Really was.*
>
> *Gordon Painter:*
> *It was lovely. That's a super looking ship. And it looked vast in my eyes, that's a vast thing. These days, when one looks at it, it looks reasonably small, but alongside some of the other ones. But to me it looked large. I feel very honoured to have been part of it and doing my best for what we all know was a good cause, and I shall never forget it. She's a lovely ship.*
>
> *Denis Parkinson:*
> *She was always a well-liked ship. Used to call her the Tiddly Bee because Tiddly is the term using the name, you know, being nice and good and the best. She was a lucky ship. She was very lucky in a lot of respects.*
>
> *Murray Ward:*
> *Well, the Belfast is the best one of all the ships I served on, was like one big family, was never any arguments. Had a couple of punch-ups when people come off drunk, but they never had animosity or anything like that on there.*

Belfast **arrives at her final home after passing under Tower Bridge in October 1971. (Imperial War Museum)**

World of Warships is a free-to-play, naval warfare–themed, massively multiplayer online game produced and published by Wargaming. As in their other games, *World of Tanks* (WoT) and *World of Warplanes* (WoWP), players take control of historic vehicles to battle others in player-vs-player battles or play cooperatively against bots in a player-vs-environment (PvE) mode. *World of Warships* (WoWS) was originally released for PCs in 2015 and was followed in 2018 by a mobile adaptation, *World of Warships Blitz*. The PlayStation 4 and Xbox One console version, titled *World of Warships: Legends*, released in 2019 and became available on PlayStation 5 and Xbox Series X/S in April 2021.

Developed by Wargaming d.o.o. in Belgrade, Serbia, *World of Warships* (PC) currently has millions of registered players—playing on four main servers across the globe. More than 500 dedicated staff members work on a four-week update cycle to bring new features, ships, and mechanics to the game—keeping gameplay fresh and inviting to new players. The game features more than 700 ships, spread across 13 different in-game nations. Ships are designed based on historical documents and actual blueprints from the first half of the twentieth century, and it takes from two to six months on average to create each of these ships. There are more than 23 ports to choose from, and 16 of them are re-created based on historic harbors and port towns.

There are five different ship classes—destroyers, cruisers, battleships, aircraft carriers, and submarines—with each class offering a different gameplay experience. Ships are arranged in tiers between I and X, plus so-called superships, which represent the pinnacle of naval engineering from World War II and the early Cold War era. Players must progress through ship classes and tiers to reach tier X, after which they get access to these behemoths. Each warship needs a naval commander to lead it into battle, and there are many commanders to choose from in *World of Warships*, including more than 15 iconic historical figures. In *World of Warships*, players can battle on more than 40

THE DISTINGUISHED SERVICE ORDER

The Distinguished Service Order was established in 1886 by Queen Victoria to be awarded to officers for distinguised service during active operations. A cross-shaped order was made of white enamel and was ornamented by the Imperial Crown surrounded by a laurel wreath. The cross was worn with a red ribbon with blue stripes that was also decorated with laurel leaves.

For his contribution to the victory in the Battle of the North Cape, where Royal Navy ships hunted down and sank the German Battleship *Scharnhorst*, Captain Frederick Parham of HMS *Belfast* was awarded the Distinguished Service Order.

maps. There are seven different permanent or seasonal Battle Types to choose from, including Co-op Battles, Random Battles, Ranked Battles, Clan Battles, Brawls, and Scenarios. From time to time, additional Special Event Battles are held.

HMS *Belfast* was originally represented in World of Warships at Tier VII, first being offered for sale as a premium ship in the fall of 2016. This postwar version of the ship was permanently removed from sale shortly after and is now only available via containers. In 2020, *Belfast* returned in her World War II configuration, as *Belfast* '43 at Tier VIII. Neither version is available for sale, though the Tier VIII *Edinburgh*, which *Belfast* is a sister of, is available to research in the light cruiser branch of the Royal Navy tech tree.

Developed by the team behind *World of Warships* for PC, *World of Warships: Legends* is a different entry in Wargaming's flagship nautical franchise that takes full advantage of the power and capabilities of home consoles. *World of Warships: Legends* brings the online naval action loved by millions to home consoles for the very first time, alongside a host of content and features exclusive to the console experience. *World of Warships: Legends* is now available to download from the PlayStation® Store and Microsoft Store. Players can now wage wars across a variety of maps, in numerous warships, and enjoy stunning oceanic vistas with glorious HDR support on PlayStation®4 and Xbox One X. Full 4K support is available on PlayStation®4 Pro and PlayStation®5, and Xbox One X too! *Legends* also supports standard high-def on PlayStation®4 and Xbox One, with more intriguing graphics on the horizon.

BADGE OF CRUISER BELFAST

HMS *Belfast*, commisioned in 1939, belongs to the last series of Town-class light cruisers. The ship's badge features a mythological animal, the Hippocampus (seahorse), derived from the Coat of Arms of the city of Belfast, after which the cruiser was named.
At the Battle of the North Cape, HMS *Belfast* was the flagship of the 10th Cruiser Squadron commanded by Vice Admiral Robert Burnett. *Belfast* was first to make radar contact with *Scharnhorst* and later took the lead in the pursuit of the German battleship.

Wargaming proudly supports various charitable causes that members of the gaming and history community care for deeply:

Supporting veterans and servicemembers

- Operation Lifeboat (2020) raised $150,000 USD for Stack Up's mental health awareness helpline.
- Remembrance charity drive (2020) raised $45,000 USD for Help for Heroes, which supports UK veterans and service members.
- Project Valor (2017) saw *WoWS*, *WoT*, and *WoWP* raising $75,000 USD for a veteran housing program.

In 1971, HMS *Belfast* was saved from scrapping and preserved as a museum ship, opening to the public on the Thames near Tower Bridge. As a museum, it provides visitors with a unique opportunity to explore a historic warship, offering insights into naval warfare, life at sea, and the broader history of the twentieth century. The ship is preserved to reflect different periods of its operational history, including areas such as the captain's bridge, engine rooms, gun turrets, and sailors' living quarters. Interactive exhibits and multimedia displays help bring the ship's stories to life, allowing visitors to experience the daily routines and challenges faced by the crew.

One of the highlights is The Command Centre, which is a fully equipped interactive gaming room in the heart of the ship. Using a specially prepared build of the online naval action video game *World of Warships*, you can take the virtual helm of the very Royal Navy cruiser you are standing in and lead her into battle.

HMS *Belfast* is not only a historical artifact but also an educational resource, offering educational programs and guided tours that provide deeper historical context and engage audiences of all ages. It serves as a reminder of the courage and sacrifices made by those who served on board and in the Royal Navy.

Today, HMS *Belfast* continues to inspire visitors by preserving and sharing its rich history, making the cruiser one of the most fascinating and educational museum experiences in London.

WORLD OF WARSHIPS
LEGENDS
IWM
WORLD OF WARSHIPS
IWM
WORLD OF
WARSHIPS
IWM

GAS
WORLD OF WARSHIPS
Continue the fun at home! Play for free on PC
at warships.co.uk to gain access to exclusive content!
WORLD OF
WARSHIPS
IWM
IMPERIAL WAR MUSEUMS
PLAY FOR FREE AT
warships.co.uk

WORLD OF
WARSHIPS
IWM
IMPERIAL WAR MUSEUMS
PLAY FOR FREE AT

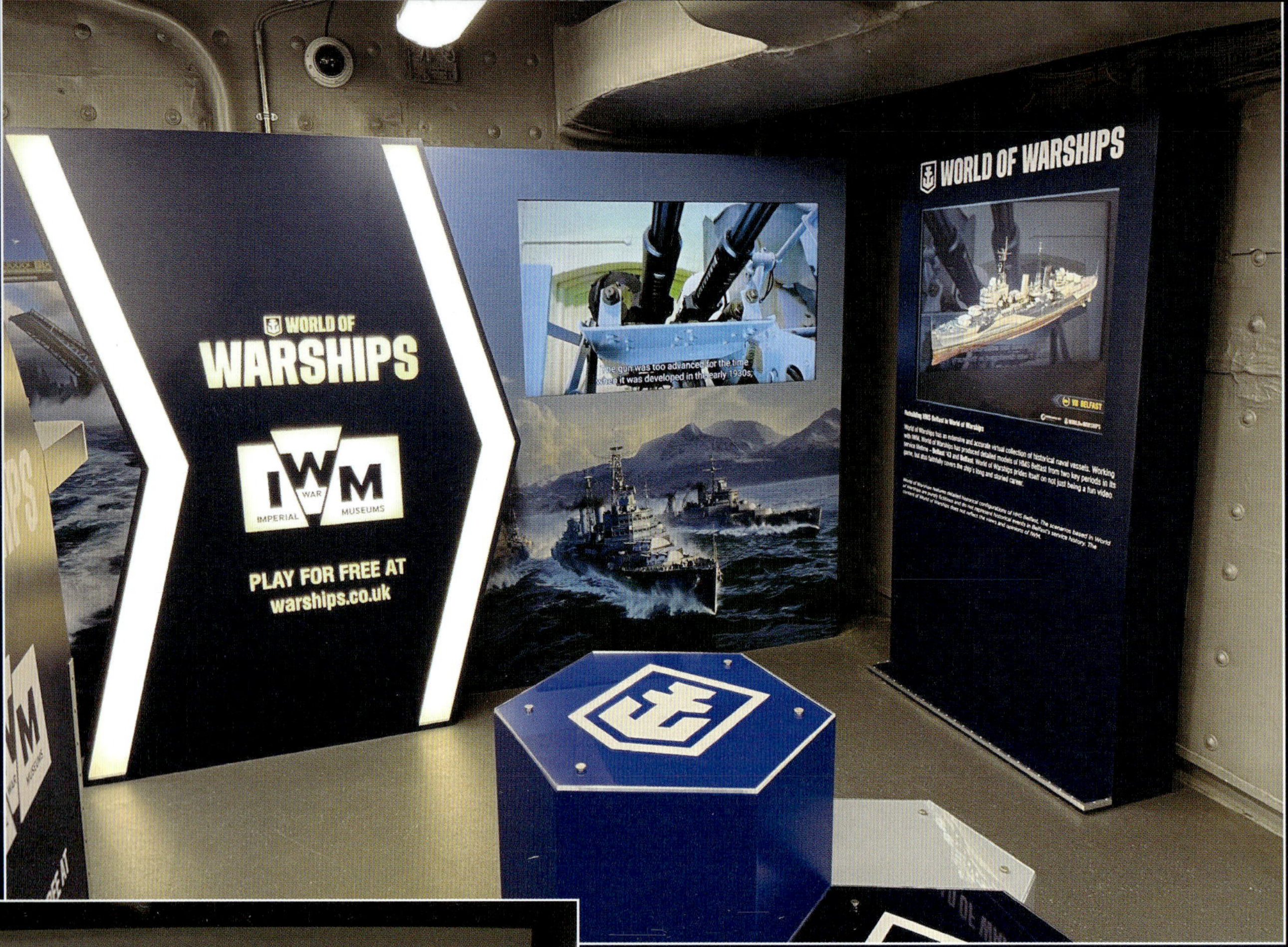
WORLD OF
WARSHIPS
IWM
WAR
IMPERIAL
MUSEUMS
PLAY FOR FREE AT
warships.co.uk
WORLD OF WARSHIPS

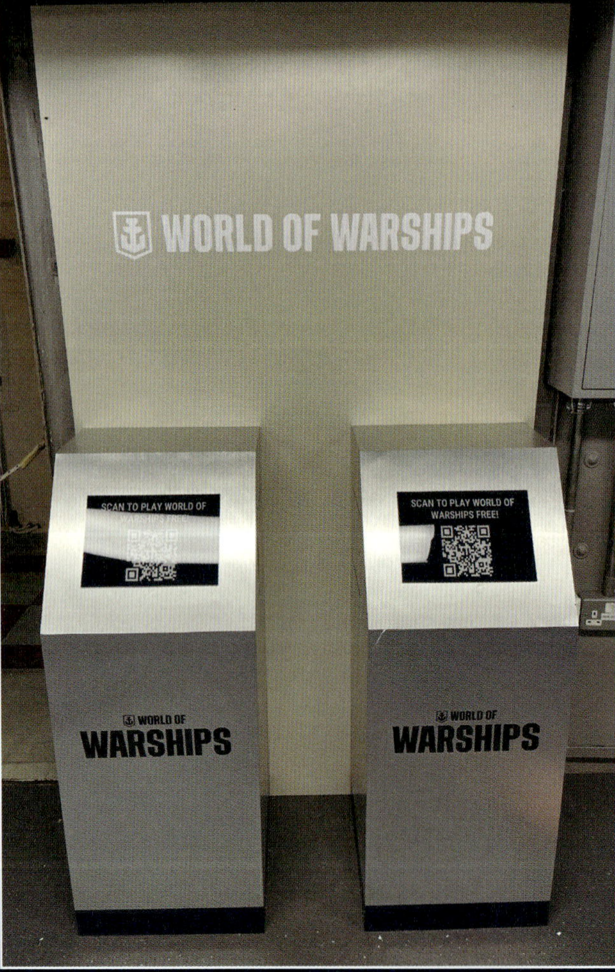

WORLD OF WARSHIPS
SCAN TO PLAY WORLD OF WARSHIPS FREE!
WORLD OF
WARSHIPS
WORLD OF
WARSHIPS

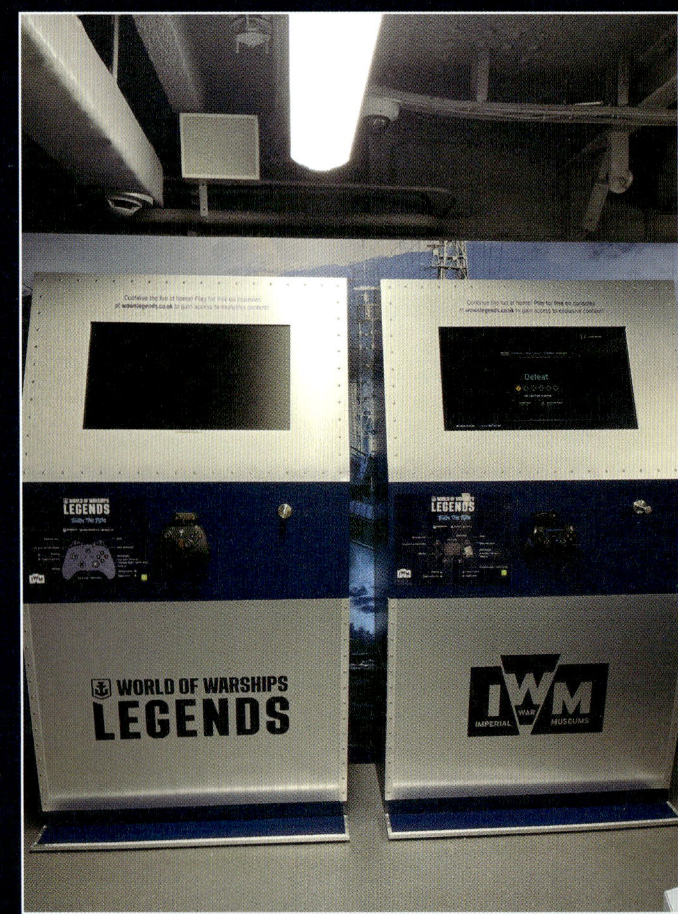

WORLD OF WARSHIPS
LEGENDS
IWM
WAR
IMPERIAL
MUSEUMS